THE ART OF HIGH ENERGY

The Art of High Energy

VANDA MARTIN

LIONCREST
PUBLISHING

THE ART OF HIGH ENERGY

ISBN   978-1-61961-858-9 *Paperback*

978-1-61961-857-2 *Ebook*

To my mom and dad, Lourdes and Ivon, for teaching me the energy of love, patience, hard work and strength. I miss you two!

To my wonderful sons, Peter and Ivon, for inspiring and motivating me to be the best mom and person I can be. I love you both immensely!

To my partner in crime and adventure, Jesse. Thank you for being there for me, even when I go dreaming away on my unicorn.

Contents

——

Foreword

BY TOM FERRY

I have a long history with Vanda Martin.

But for quite some time, I didn't realize all the different things she has accomplished in her life.

She's been a bar owner, a restaurant owner, an importer/ exporter, a retail store operator and owner, a basketball player, a personal trainer, a model—as well as an ultra-successful real estate professional, great team leader, and a powerful real estate coach.

Highly impressive!

Here's the funny part:

If you've ever met Vanda, none of this is surprising in any way.

She's overflowing with infectious energy.

She knows how to channel that energy into positive results.

And most importantly, Vanda doesn't take her natural energy for granted, she works on it constantly and consistently.

She recognizes it's more than a gift, and she's figured out a way to share that gift with others.

That's what this book is all about.

I'm honored she asked me to write this foreword because as a real estate coach and owner of the industry's leading coaching company, my whole purpose is putting people into positive action.

Vanda's obvious ability to do exactly that on a daily basis is her key to success, and she's now sharing that key with you.

If you're looking to up your energy game, I highly recommend you pay attention to every word in this book. Vanda knows how to tap into and expand people's energy, allowing them to perform at higher levels and achieve greater overall fulfillment in their lives.

Whether or not you were born with the gift of natural energy, you'll learn how to adopt a mindset for success and bring increased action to your life. The more you put yourself into positive action, the more improvement, growth, and prosperity you will achieve.

TOM FERRY

Founder and CEO, Tom Ferry International

#1 Real Estate Educator by Swanepoel Power 200 and bestselling author of *Life! By Design* and *Mindset, Model and Marketing*

Introduction

"The higher your energy level, the more efficient your body. The more efficient your body, the better you feel, and the more you will use your talents to produce outstanding results."
—TONY ROBBINS

High energy is a hot commodity. Everyone wants more energy, so they can do more and be more. High energy is so desirable that you can find thousands of different types of products all claiming to give you that desired boost of energy. There are pills, herbs, drinks, powders, potions—you name it, it exists—all claiming to deliver the energy you need to become your best self.

But, you can't buy your way to higher energy. Energy is something you work on; it's not something you just have. We're not given energy at birth. It's not owed to us. It's not a gift we should expect to materialize. Energy is something we create and grow only if we put in the effort through a combination of right actions.

What are these "right actions?" They are how we think, how we move, what we focus on, how we act, how we dream, how we feel, what we eat and drink, and how we breathe. When you couple these right actions with a positive mindset, you can create and keep the high energy you desire to take you further in life.

"Energy" comes from the Greek word *energia*, which means "active work." Energy is the fuel of life that keeps us moving and active. Energy flows through us like water flows through a riverbed.

We are made of pure energy. We vibrate waves of energy just like a microwave, or the way a cell phone does. The waves are undetectable, but they are always transmitting. The energy we radiate can be positive, negative, or neutral. We have various types of energy: the energy we create by physical motion, and the energy we send out by our thoughts and feelings.

Through productive mental and physical engagement, we create energy. When you're engaged, you're open to receiving good, positive emotion. When you receive positive emotion, you feel connected. When you feel connected, your mind, body, and soul are acting, and that action creates energy. Getting yourself engaged even in one area will help engage all other areas of your life. For instance, when I see someone who is tired or a little down, I tell them to put their body into motion to create good energy, and then their mind and soul will follow.

To create or improve energy, we all must first decide that we want to do it. We have the choice to generate, improve, multiply, or expand our energy. When we decide to grow our energy, we can live a high-energy life.

What Is High Energy?

Someone who has high energy is happy with what they have. They are grateful. They are joyful and at peace with themselves.

People with high energy will exercise, drink water, eat properly, and breathe well.

Those with high energy dream more and believe they can have what they want if they are committed to getting it. They understand that what they focus on dictates their thoughts. That, in turn, impacts their emotions. Their emotions determine their general attitudes, and their attitudes create their behaviors.

How High Energy Changes Your Life

High energy makes you happier and keeps your body stronger. It helps you become resilient and heal, both mentally and physically. It makes you healthier. It brings you joy. It gives you enthusiasm and vitality. You have a lighter disposition, a robust underlying strength, and an optimistic point of view.

When you're optimistic, you expect good things. When you expect good things, you commit longer to whatever you are trying to accomplish, because you believe it will work out for the best.

Usually, when you have high energy, you have more faith. The Bible tells us that faith moves mountains. So, if we use faith and optimism to direct our high energy, we can move mountains and obstacles to make things happen.

One of the Best Things about Having High Energy

The more energy you have, the more you can use that energy to help you focus. This focus, in turn, creates more energy. It becomes a self-fulfilling process.

People around you can feel it. They will feel your energy field and your aura. People love being around others who have high, clean, pure emotion and who are calm, peaceful, and strong.

All of us have one thing in common—we only have twenty-four hours in a day. The president, the CEO of Google, you, and I all have twenty-four hours each day. We have a finite amount of time. But, what we do with that time changes dramatically from person to person. The more energy you have, the more you can do with those twenty-four hours.

When you have high energy, you can work at peak performance, and you can accomplish more in less time. You can become more efficient and effective. You can accomplish more than the average person can.

With the right strategies, focus, resources, and determination, anyone can create more energy to live a fuller life and find success. I did it and so can you.

The Beginning of My Energy Journey

I first became aware of the power of energy when I was very young. My mother and father separated when I was ten years old. When I was twelve years old, I started to notice my mother was really struggling financially and emotionally. She had to work long hours, sometimes at three different jobs to take care of us. My father helped but it was not enough. I saw how hard that was for her. So, during those moments, I decided I was never going to depend on anyone. I was going to be rich so I could support my mother and give her the gift of financial security.

I knew education was very important for success, so I launched into my studies. I became a bookworm—a little bit of a geek—and I even had very thick glasses! All I wanted to do was read and read about three books a week. I mostly read books that were inspirational and adventurous, but also liked to read mysteries and fantasies, because I dreamt of an escape. Those years were difficult for us; we moved around a lot. In twelve months, we moved twice.

During those unstable years, I started to observe people who were successful. I noticed that people who were successful all had one thing in common—a trait I didn't know how to describe. They were unusually spirited, strong, and powerful. They were cool and composed, and my goodness, they all smiled a lot. It also seemed like they had a good amount of knowledge.

I settled on the word "charisma" to describe people like that. But that word didn't exactly explain what I felt when I watched them. What they had was so much more than that. It was almost like an aura that made people become attracted to them.

What was it? I asked myself this question countless times.

Then, one day, I understood. They had high energy! They vibrated at a different frequency than everyone else. They were magnetic. Their power was undeniable. Their energy was contagious! I decided I wanted to be like that. After that epiphany, I told myself, "From now on, I will become a student of energy and success. I will operate on their level. I will be better and produce more."

I've been thinking about, working on, dreaming about, and studying energy since that time. My high energy didn't come to me all at once. I worked on growing my energy over the course of many years. Only after some time did anyone mention that they noticed a difference in me.

By the time I was nineteen, I was going to university, taking French classes, and I was officially the owner of a successful bar. People began noticing my work habits— how I was able to do it all—and they asked me what my secrets were. They wanted to know where I got my energy from, and they even asked if I could bottle it up and sell it to them! Those comments made me happy and I felt like I was finally on my way; but still, I wanted more energy. I looked at my early success in business and while at university. Then, I thought to myself, *You're not done. You can do more. You can be more energetic.*

That was when I decided to do whatever it took to grow my energy with intention and purpose.

Since then, my high energy has brought me success. I've

learned three languages, founded and run four of my own businesses, and I've raised two incredible kids. I want to be clear; I was not born with the high energy that helps me achieve so much. I invested my time, and I worked hard to multiply my energy. Never once have I taken this for granted, nor have I ever rested on my laurels. I've always stayed humble and worked hard.

On my path, I have always worked diligently to curate my high energy—ever since that realization in the bar.

The Path toward Energy

I was born and raised in Brazil and finished university at a young age. I loved Brazil, but I wanted to move to Lyon, France, to get a master's degree in business. Before I flew to France, I decided to visit San Francisco with my sister for a month. On the plane ride from Rio to Miami, I met my now ex-husband. When we met, I spoke Portuguese and French, but no English. We courted past our language barrier, he in Los Angeles and I in San Francisco. Then, instead of moving to France, I moved to Los Angeles and we married a year later.

While in Southern California, I learned English. I was admitted to the University of California, Los Angeles, to work on my specialization in business and management.

Around the same time, I started working out at a gym in Santa Monica. Being a former basketball player, I always loved exercising and went to the gym every day. One day, the owner came up to me and told me that everyone at the gym loved my energy and my smile. He asked me if I would come work for him.

I said, "I'm going to school, but what do you have in mind?"

He told me he'd send me to school to get my certificate as a personal trainer if I promised to work for him at least part-time.

I told him, "I'm in."

So, I worked part-time as a personal trainer while I went to UCLA.

Shortly after, my husband and I moved to Marin County in Northern California where we had my first son, Peter. Later, my husband got a job in the Central Valley of California, so we moved there. By that time, I was pregnant with my second child, Ivon. It was difficult to be a new mom in a new city. I didn't know anyone, but thank God, I had my mom to help me at that time!

When my sons were very young, I was a full-time mom

and I loved it. But I loved business, too. I soon became restless and was anxious to start working.

At the time, the internet had just started to take off, and so I opened an import and export business. I also launched a party supply store in Northeast Brazil, which allowed me to import and export my own products. Unfortunately, the party supply store was not a great idea. As you can imagine, it is difficult to manage a retail operation from overseas.

I decided to close that business and pursue something I had always loved from a young age—real estate. I loved selling, but I especially loved selling big-ticket items. So, real estate seemed the perfect fit. What was bigger than a house? It sure beat selling balloons!

I got my real estate license when my boys were still young, and I went to work for Coldwell Banker.

As a realtor, I had to give my potential clients something we call a listing presentation. During a listing presentation, I would explain to potential clients how I planned to sell their home. Every time I conducted a listing presentation, I was basically interviewing for a job. Imagine interviewing for a job every single day!

When my clients hired me as their realtor to list their house, I always asked them one question: "Why did you choose to work with Vanda Martin?" I knew they had many choices of realtors to work with—every market has thousands of realtors, and the competition is always fierce.

More times than I can count, I have heard, "You and your competition have a lot of knowledge and plenty of skill and experience. But, what I like about you is your energy and enthusiasm. We want someone with that great energy selling our house."

Time and time again, my energy has helped me win clients. They were attracted to my enthusiasm, engagement, passion, conviction, and confidence...all the result of my high energy.

Over the years, I have been asked how I achieve and maintain my high energy. I share my secrets openly and willingly with the people around me. I want everyone to be able to achieve high energy that will transform people's lives. That's why I wrote this book!

Teachings

In this book, I will teach you how to achieve and maintain high energy. You will learn:

1. Ways to create and maximize your energy level
2. How to be aware of your energy power

3. Strategies to strengthen your willpower and mindset
4. How to create positive habits through discipline, focus, and persistence
5. Why energy can help you do more so you can be more
6. How to optimize mental, spiritual, and physical energy
7. Ways to understand the parts that work together to make us who we are, including our thoughts, actions, and feelings

How to Use Energy to Enhance Your Life

As someone learning the art of applying energy to your life, you should:

1. Be inspired by my examples
2. Follow the easy steps provided
3. Have fun and spread joy
4. Take notes on what you must implement
5. Implement the changes

Follow the Leader

My goal is to help you obtain the same level of high energy that I've created for myself.

As you read through this book, you will work on strategies to redirect your energy, change your mindset, and take action to achieve the life you dream of.

As a coach, I work with high-performing people who want to do more while also finding balance in their lives. Every person can start fresh and reboot their life and have the energy level they want.

SECTION I

Energy Mindset

CHAPTER 1

Release Energy Blocks

———

"The energy of the mind is the essence of life."
—ARISTOTLE

Have you ever encountered someone you just really liked or loved immediately? There was just something about that person—a vibration maybe, an aura, charisma, or some sort of beautiful energy field—that just made you light up.

You might have had trouble describing it, but whatever it was, it was a combination of pure love, joy, hope, compassion, and all the other clean, high emotions that made you want to be around that person. We all love being around people like that.

You felt that person's energy, and it attracted you to them—not in a sexual way, but as if you were vibrating on the same wavelength. You felt connected. You felt the vibes. You were emitting the same energy, and it made you feel more connected to them.

We all have energy that either attracts people or repels people. Everyone has a certain vibration. We can't see our vibrations, nor can we feel them. But, other people and the universe receive our vibrations and are affected by them.

Energy Types

There are four types of energy:

- Mental energy
- Emotional energy
- Physical energy
- Spiritual energy

There is also a special fifth energy called personal energy. Your personal energy is your personal vibration; it is the mixture of all of the other energies. It's what makes you *you*. It's what makes me *me*. This energy is your magnetic vibration, your aura, your light. It enables you to be more productive and active, and it drives your life force. You can't see it, but everyone around you can feel it.

Energy Field

Your energy field surrounds you at all times. Your state of mind and the rate at which your energy vibrates controls your state. Your energy field can be strong or weak depending on what level of energy you're vibrating at.

It's possible for your energy field to get stronger and weaker depending on what's happening in your life. There are entities that can contaminate and deplete your energy. Negative emotions drain you. Fear, resentment, jealousy, envy, anger, regret, hate, and guilt all have the ability to weaken your energy field. They act like vampires, sucking the energy right out of you! If you are dealing with these types of emotions, they will slow down the vibration of your energy field.

On the other hand, there are emotions like joy, love, faith, compassion, and gratitude. These emotions bolster your energy field. They make you calmer, more powerful, and more resourceful. Your vibrations become more magnetic, and they vibrate at a faster frequency. The faster they vibrate, the stronger you are.

Magnetic Vibrations

What are magnetic vibrations? Think again about your impression when meeting someone fabulous for the first time. You feel their positive energy vibration. You sense that high energy we all want to have.

High vibration energies come from a combination of high physical, mental, and spiritual energies. It's as powerful as high-octane fuel!

People with high energy move through life with power and intention. They are graceful and usually have a spark. They can do more than most. They have more intention, which brings them more clarity. They emit a stronger magnetism that pulls good things toward them. They have the internal power to recover faster from life's curveballs—they are resilient. They're happier and live longer! Who doesn't want that? There are studies that say happy people live seven to ten years longer than those who are unhappy.

What about the case where you meet someone who just rubs you the wrong way? That person has a negative energy vibration. They are repelling you instead of drawing you closer.

Their low vibration energies push you away.

Energy Blocks

At times, our energy levels can suffer because of something I call energy blocks.

Energy blocks are like the kinks that sometimes get into garden hoses, preventing you from watering your plants. Water is trying to flow, but can't because there is a blockage—so it starts to back up. If there is too much pressure, the hose can rupture.

Energy blocks, like kinks in hoses, prevent energy from flowing. Ultimately, these energy blocks diminish the strength of your vibrations. They can originate from the tragedy and trauma we all endure as humans.

One of my best friends lost her father in an unexpected accident. Her shock caused a major energy block to the point where she had a terrible migraine and went blind for two days.

Energy blocks also come from the baggage we carry in our life—past abuses, ordeals, or trials. They also come from the heavy emotions we refuse to get rid of, such as anger, hate, resentment, fear, envy, jealousy, regret, shame, and guilt. They all act as energy blocks.

When energy blocks stay in place long enough, bad things can happen. Your immune system drops, and you can open yourself up to becoming sick. Some believe that common ailments such as arthritis, cancer, back problems, neck problems, shivers, aches, tight muscles, shallow breathing, fatigue, and other illnesses come from energy blocks like stress and anger. Too much stress triggers cortisol releases, which have negative long-term effects. Some believe these blocks can weaken our bodies at the cellular level, which results in mutations and damaged DNA, leading to harmful health problems down the line.

I believe when you have energy blocks, you become more prone to having accidents because you are out of focus and out of sync.

When energy blocks are not released, you lose out on experiencing joy. Your energy waves slow down, vibrations dwindle, and your energy field breaks. Most importantly, they block positive emotions from reaching you.

The Role of Your Mind

I'm a believer that your outlook on life is comprised of two things. Ninety percent of your outlook is based on how you perceive and filter the world. The other 10 percent comes from your circumstance. Even if your environment is bad, you can change your outlook to have a positive mindset. Your mindset is powerful. You can choose to see the world in an optimistic way or in a pessimistic way.

You create your own reality. You can create a self-fulfilling prophecy. If all you think about is the negative, you carry that baggage wherever you go. You can be carrying a beautiful Louis Vuitton bag, but if it is full of negativity, regret, and pain, it won't look very good.

Many people have a nasty habit of worrying too much. But, does worrying help in any way? No! Worrying drains your energy. It's the opposite of productive! It doesn't make anything better; it makes things *worse*. Not only does it drain your energy, it makes you less empowered. It takes away clarity and brings fear to your life. Ultimately, it stops you from acting.

When you worry, your mind blocks the good energy! How do we get around this? We change our state of mind by changing our focus and our thoughts.

It's very difficult to control those negative thoughts that just pop up in our minds. Sometimes, a negative thought will just hit you out of the blue! We can't choose them or protect against them; they just happen. But, we can decide not to follow the negative thoughts.

If you can stop the second, third, or fourth thoughts in their tracks, you can break the negative cycle of worrying. Worrying is not productive, it's not cost-effective, it doesn't take you anywhere, and it drains your energy like nothing else can. People who worry age themselves. They always have low energy.

The moment in which you halt that second, third, or fourth thought is what I call a "recovery moment." When you break yourself from this worrying or negative-thought cycle, you gift yourself with the ability to shift your energy.

Let's say you're constantly worrying about a negative situation with your daughter who is struggling in school. Perhaps you think about her all the time. During nearly every free moment in your day, a worrisome thought about your daughter pops into your head. Normally, you would engage that thought, give it attention, and let it feed on your energy. You might spend dozens of minutes ruminating on that thought, but worrying about it won't help. Work on the solution, not the worry.

We think about sixty to eighty thousand thoughts a day. Studies have shown that 75 to 80 percent of those thoughts are negative. That's a lot of opportunity for negative thoughts to take hold of your brain. But, it's also an opportunity to think positive thoughts. You've got to develop the mental discipline of replacing the negative with the positive, and then take action immediately. When you take action through physical activity, you can engage your mind. If you keep yourself busy and engaged in positive action, then you won't have time to worry.

This positive energy will vibrate out into the universe. It

will bounce, skip, and travel throughout, and your energy blocks will clear up.

Energy blocks really hinder the mind, even if all your other energies are flowing. The mind, spinning and spinning, will drain your energy and slow you down, even if you are physically fit and eating healthy.

Clearing the Mind and Body So Energy Can Flow

I often work through clearing energy blocks with my clients. I've seen many types of blocks, and I've learned how to help my clients free themselves from all negative thoughts. I want to share how we work through them.

First, I tell my clients to relax when they get home. Truly relax. I ask them to do some breathing. I ask them to quiet their minds and search for the negative feeling or emotion that is affecting them.

I ask them to describe their emotions and write them down. We must identify whatever it is and put it on paper.

We work together to see what causes those negative emotions. We explore whether their emotions are based on realities or just their perception of reality. Most of the time, our pain comes from memories or stories that taunt us as we think about them over and over, like a broken record.

We get stuck. We can't grow, and we surely can't get better while running the same old sad story through our heads.

I ask my clients to ask themselves:

1. Is what you're thinking and feeling true? Is the story in your head really true?
2. Do you have proof of that?
3. What is the cost of those beliefs on you and your family on a daily basis?
4. What could you do or be if you could just get rid of that story or self-limiting belief?

Then, I ask them to visualize themselves as free from that story and their emotional burdens. I ask my clients to say to themselves, "This happened a long time ago. It's not who I am anymore."

Then, I ask them to release it by forgiving themselves or the person the feeling is directed toward. There is an energy of forgiveness that comes from forgiving and forgetting. This energy leads to rejuvenation and aids in decontamination.

Next, I ask them to create a ceremony by burning the list or ripping it up to celebrate the fact that the old "you" is gone.

Often, it takes time to release these energy blocks. It takes practice and determination, so don't feel discouraged if it doesn't happen for you immediately.

But, with enough determination, you can accomplish this quickly.

With my clients, we work on strategies to clear those energy blocks, so they can produce more. When we can release our old negative or self-limiting beliefs, we can forgive ourselves and free ourselves of our negative energy. The liberation that comes from the release of negative feelings is one of the best feelings in the world. It gives us the power and permission to start fresh.

If the Blocks Come Back

Create an anchor.

What do I mean by an anchor? Well, what does an anchor do for a boat? It holds the boat in place and out of danger of getting lost. The anchor gives the boat security, support, and a sense of groundedness in the middle of the sea. Without the anchor, who knows what trouble that boat might get into?

The anchor helps keep us from drifting into an old mindset. It helps keep us from running ashore.

Anchors are important. The anchor acts as a police force in

our heads, preventing us from allowing negativity, doubt, fear, blame, and guilt into our recovery process while we grow new habits. Think about it. The normal forty-year-old person has thirty-five years of habits ingrained within himself—mentally, physically, and emotionally. Some people habitually return to a negative thought process when there is any sign of trouble on their horizon. The pull of negative energy is strong, and they have a tendency to go back to their old selves. It can be easy to fall back into old habits.

Starting new habits means we have to go through the process of habit creation. We can create habits in as fast as thirty days, but IT CAN TAKE ABOUT NINETY DAYS to create a STRONG habit. It all depends on how disciplined you are.

When you feel like you are slipping back into your old habits, go to a quiet place.

Close your eyes. Remember how you felt when you had a moment of success. Remember how wonderful you felt. Remember how your high emotions made you optimistic. Recall the emotion of high energy and how that feeling drove your positive change in behavior and attitude.

Go back to that moment when you won and felt absolutely on top of the world. You don't have to recreate the ritual, but you must recreate the feeling. Sourcing this powerful memory will give you the energy you need to move on when you're struggling.

Get your body into action. Your mind will follow.

If all else fails and your mental, physical, or emotional energy stalls, have a plan in place to reignite yourself to get back into the right energy. Get moving! Go outside! Go for a run. Walk your dog. Go dancing. Make some calls! Your physical energy will raise and then your personal energy will follow.

This plan is akin to memorizing a play in sports. When I played basketball, our coach taught us plays that helped set us up for success. We could rely on that plan to set us up to win. Apply that idea to your life. Have a play in your playbook that you can fall back on when times get tough. Think of it as your secret weapon, or your cape.

The Most Common Energy Block

Fear is the most common and the most devastating energy block, because it can pop up in many areas of your life. You can suffer from fear of success, fear of failure, fear of intimacy, fear of being alone, fear of rejection, fear of love...the list goes on.

After we meet our physiological needs, the number one

thing humans need is belonging. We need to feel acknowledged, loved, important, and connected. That's why social media is such a phenomenon. It allows people to feel instantaneously connected.

If we don't deal with our fear, we will never be able to have peace of mind or high focus and calm energy.

No matter what happens in your life, you have to address fear. Fear is everywhere, but when we face it, its power dissipates. Courageous people aren't courageous because they have no fear. They do have fear. They just confront it.

You can't afford fear. It kills you little by little, every day. It takes your joy away from you. Which, if you think about it, is ridiculous. On average, only 3 to 4 percent of our fears actually manifest in any real way.

It's important to practice releasing fear. By following a recovery plan, you can change your state of mind and get away from the fear.

You can develop a resilient, disciplined, persistent, and consistent state of mind that blocks against stupid, disempowering, negative thoughts that control your reality. Resilience is important because it enables you to pop right back up from obstacles. Persistence keeps you in the game—no matter what's going on, you can stay in the fight. Consistency helps you do it over and over, day in and day out. Discipline keeps you focused and strong.

Add enthusiasm and a great attitude to this mixture and, even if you lose everything, you will have the resources to recover.

Be willing to start over; it's a beautiful freedom. No matter what, we are not stuck. Feeling stuck and helpless sucks the energy right out of us; it's one of the worst energy vampires. When people feel they have no options, they feel disempowered. When they feel stuck in their job or a relationship, it feels terrible! It drains your energy.

As Jim Rohn, one of my favorite motivational speakers, said, "If you don't like how things are, change it. You are not a tree."

You are not rooted to where you are. You are free to move, change, get up, or leave if you want! Nothing is holding you down except yourself.

You have the power to change and move.

I remind myself of that every day. Each day, I start from zero. Whatever happened in the past has nothing to do with today. I give myself permission to start new, fresh, and renewed. Giving myself permission to start over every day prevents me from feeling helpless or stuck. That gives me strength and energy.

More Than Just an Energy Block

I am not in la-la land. I understand there are cases where improving your habits to clear up energy blocks is just not enough. Sometimes, you need to see a doctor. If you are chemically imbalanced, have thyroid problems, have a health problem, or are clinically depressed, that is another situation entirely. If you are living with a physiological problem, then using the suggestions in this book will not be enough. Certainly, they will help to an extent. But, just changing your mindset will not help clear energy blocks and negative energy caused by medical problems.

After Release

After you release the energy blocks, energy can flow. Just like water that is freed from a kink in a garden hose, your energy will flow steadfast. Your determination, stamina, enthusiasm, and passion will flow as well. There will be no constriction.

At this point, you will be able to create space to add more positive things to your life. Now that you've learned how to get rid of your energy blocks, we'll explore how to change negative energy into positive energy.

CHAPTER 2

Change Your Energy

———

"You are what you think about most of the time."
—EARL NIGHTINGALE

To achieve success in all or any areas of your life, you first have to learn how to reprogram your mindset.

Law of Attraction

The law of attraction states that you attract what you think about most of the time. This law proves itself true all the time in my life.

Have you ever had a situation where you thought about something, and then it happened?

For instance, let's say I've been thinking about getting a new car: a black BMW Convertible. Suddenly, I start noticing black BMW Convertibles everywhere I go. How is this possible? It's not as if 25 percent of the population suddenly woke up one morning and all went out to buy black BMW Convertibles. So, why am I seeing them all over town, out of the blue?

Our brain filters millions of stimuli every day. It does this in large part to keep us safe. Normally, my brain wouldn't take note of black BMW Convertibles, but because I've put in my mind that I want to get one, my brain is now hardwired to filter them into my consciousness. This filter is called the reticular activated system (RAS). The RAS filters in important stimuli and filters out unimportant stimuli.

So, because I'm thinking of black BMW Convertibles, I'm now taking note of them and they suddenly seem to be everywhere!

Our brains are the most amazing computers on the planet. Every thought you have is like a piece of code that becomes embedded in the functions of your brain. Our thoughts become like the software running a computer. The more I program in thoughts about black BMW Convertibles, the more I encounter them in my daily life.

When I was selling real estate, Friday afternoons when I finished up early, I would get into my convertible and drive around looking for "For Sale by Owner" houses.

At one point in my life, I lived in this beautiful gated country club. Many Fridays, I would also just ride around saying, "Hello," to my neighbors. I loved enjoying those sunny days. Where I lived was so beautiful. There was just one nice, expensive, house after another.

I have a very cool story from this time. One Friday afternoon, I took a drive with my convertible top down. I put my hand up in the air, and I said to myself, "What a beautiful day. Look at these gorgeous houses on the golf course. I'm selling them all." I raised my hand higher into the air as an affirmation. I felt powerful, strong, and positive. Again, I said, "I'm selling all these beautiful homes on the golf course. I'm selling them all!"

I finished my nice drive and went home. Five minutes after I walked inside the house, I heard a knock on the door. I went to the door, opened it, and saw my neighbor standing there. She asked me if I could talk and I said, "Sure!"

"I want you to meet my friend. She lives on the ninth hole, but she just bought a new house and is going to move down to Newport Beach. She wants to sell her house here. I told her she had to go with you because you're wonderful, you do a great job, and you've got what it takes!"

I sent over the contracts, and by the end of the next day, she had signed with me!

I put the property on the market, and less than ten days later, I got a call from a doctor who was interested in moving into the neighborhood. He said, "Vanda Martin." I said, "Yes?" He said, "I know you just got a listing on the golf course and I know you represent the seller, but I've heard great things about you. I want you to show me the home and, if I like it, I want to buy it."

I took him to the house, and he decided he wanted to buy.

I wrote up the paperwork, and the deal was done within three days! Because I represented the buyer and the seller, it was one of the biggest commission checks I had ever received.

I smiled at my good fortune! This all happened right after I sent my high energy out and told myself, "I'm selling all these homes!"

Now, I believe in energy, and I believe in the law of attraction. I'd sent the right commands and the right affirmations out into the world. I had programmed my brain to attract what I wanted.

Negative Energy

People who suffer from negative energy are not necessarily mean, bad, or evil people. Sometimes, people who have negative energy suffer from fear, guilt, shame, envy, constant worries, regret, and remorse. They may harbor hate, anger, resentment, and jealousy. Their low emotions drain them, slow them down, make them tired, and restrict them.

With that kind of programming, they can't be happy. Their cells don't move quickly. Their heart feels tight. They get sick often and they are tired all the time. Their body becomes polluted. They have negative attitudes, which result in damaging actions such as gossiping, criticizing, and acting arrogantly. Those actions lead them to prejudice and intolerance of others. All in all, their lives become smaller and bleak.

When I encounter a person who emits negative energy, they seem heavy, lethargic, and disempowered. I feel sad for them. I can't give them love, patience, or compassion, because they are so blocked from anger and resentment.

The worst part, you see, is that we attract what we emit. People who have negative energy attract negative energy. They are destined to tumble in a cycle of low energy.

Dr. Wayne Dyer, renowned author and speaker, once

asked, "If I were to squeeze this orange as hard as I could, what would come out? Do you think apple juice could come out of it? What about grapefruit juice? What would come out of it? Orange juice, of course. Let's assume this orange isn't an orange, but it's you. And someone squeezes you, puts pressure on you, says something you don't like, and offends you. And out of you comes anger, hatred, bitterness, and fear. Why? The answer...is because that's what's inside."

Dr. Dyer says, "When someone puts the pressure on you and out of you comes anything other than love, it's because that's what you've allowed to be inside. Once you take away all those negative things you don't want in your life and replace them with love, you'll find yourself living a highly functioning life."

If you let people be who they are, they will show you who they are.

Some time ago, I read a similar analogy that I thought was so perfect. A person is like a bag of tea—all you have to do is put them in hot water and you will see their true colors.

Highway to High Energy

The good news is you aren't stuck with low energy; you can have the high energy you want. All you have to do is simply decide you want to change your energy. Once you make that choice, then create a plan and stick to it! That doesn't mean change will happen overnight. Be patient with yourself as you create your new pattern and new story.

The Energy I Choose

I *choose* to have high energy—the energy of love, gratitude, joy, and compassion. I *embrace* those emotions, and I *work* on them to strengthen my high energy.

I *add to* my energy by spreading it to others.

I *grow* my high energy by thinking loving thoughts about others.

I *focus* on the best parts of other people. I don't ruminate on their problems.

I can't afford a single negative thought. So, when a negative thought drops into my head, I've created a practice to get rid of it fast. I picture a tennis racket and when a negative thought drops in, "Bam!" I hit that thought as far away from me as I can. Every time I hit those terrible thoughts away, my invisible tennis racket gets stronger. And every time, I can hit that thought farther and farther away.

I am not afraid to police myself! It's necessary. Many

people only police themselves on what they say, but I police myself on what I think. It's important because what I think becomes my emotion, my emotion becomes my feelings, and my feelings dictate how I act.

Choosing to throw out negative thoughts has impacted my life in such positive ways, and it can for you as well.

My life is amazing because of it.

My life has gotten better at home and work. One of my former colleagues, whom I met at my first real estate office, gave me one of the best compliments I've ever received. He told our coworkers, "Guys, you've got to watch Vanda when we're at conferences and conventions. Every time I try to find her at one of those, all I have to do is look for a gathering of people. As soon as I see one, I know Vanda is in the middle of it. She is always surrounded by half a dozen people all talking to her." My energy field is strong, and I emit high energy. People are attracted to it!

I also *rarely get sick*! My energy protects against illness and accidents.

I *find success*, just as you'll be able to do also.

Decide What You Want

Before you can be who you want or get what you want, you have to decide what you want. Decide that you want more energy, and then believe in yourself to get it. Believe that you can make it happen, and then you can develop the discipline required to create, generate, improve, and maximize energy.

Self-esteem is an important precursor for this process. More than a personality trait, self-esteem is a psychological trait that allows you to believe that what you want aligns with what you can do. It helps you believe that whatever your "it" is, "it" is possible. Self-esteem is rooted in believing in yourself. So, if your self-esteem is strong, you'll be ahead of the game already. If not, you'll have to work harder.

If you don't believe in your abilities, ask yourself what your "why" is. This will help you see how important it is to believe in yourself to get the things you desire, whether it's more time, more money, or more results.

You've got to know *why* you want high energy as much as *what* you want it for. The more clear and specific you are, the stronger your purpose and motivation will be. Purpose will fuel your belief. If you still find yourself doubting, ask yourself if your doubts are related to old stories of failure. When you find yourself confident in the decision but lacking belief, consider whether low self-esteem might be a barrier.

When you know what you want, can envision the outcome, and have a strong purpose to believe in, you'll be able to take action to commit.

Doing Energy

We need to clarify something here. Many people think they either *have* or *don't have* high energy. But, energy is not something you have or don't have. It's something you *create*. You can create a high-energy state of mind by surrounding yourself with high energy. You can wear that energy like a coat or a cape. When it's time to do energy, you put your cape on and become Super Vanda or Super You. *Creating* and *doing* energy is decisive. Putting on energy will initiate the steps that create more of the same.

Discipline for Energy

Without discipline of the mind, we have chaos and fear. Without discipline of the body, we have weakness and illness. Without discipline of the soul, we have pain and suffering. Discipline is the ability to control and direct your mind, body, and soul to do and achieve what you desire.

It's not that difficult. It's a skill you can master, and like anything worthwhile, it takes time, energy, and focus. The key is to work on it, every day, little by little. Stay in the game! You will get stronger and better at it.

When we embrace and work on our personal discipline daily, we initiate our path to energy for success.

Planning for Energy

My ex-husband and I planned our boys' activities carefully so we could set them up for success. We wanted them to have exposure to a lot of areas in life, so we got them involved early on.

We put them in swim lessons at the age of two and ski lessons at the age of three. At four, they started karate and competed at the national level for about nine years.

At seven, we put them in tennis lessons and Kumon lessons to improve their math and writing skills.

We also took them everywhere with us. They ate at nice restaurants and traveled to wonderful places.

Great planning helped us to raise open, versatile, and flexible kids. Through their various activities, they learned patience, focus, and discipline.

Now, one of my sons is a Marine. One day, I was visiting his base and his commander said, "You have raised a very strong, focused young man. Excellent job!" That was and still is one of the best compliments I have ever received.

You cannot create energy without a step-by-step plan of action. When you know what you want and why you want it (in this case, high energy), you can believe in it and commit to it—but you must have a plan first, just like we created for our boys.

The same applies to your pursuit of a powerful, high-energy life. My plan includes morning rituals that I follow every day. Yours might be different, but they should be a combination of habits to improve, grow, and expand your energy and focus to the highest levels.

Affirmation and Inspiration

My plan looks something like this: my alarm goes off at a quarter to five—no, I'm not kidding—and I do two very important things right away. I do these two things because the morning is one of the best times of the day. Your brain is relaxed and malleable after seven or eight hours of sleep and it's ready to be shaped for the day.

I capitalize on this moment by first repeating affirmations. I repeat each of the following phrases three times, "Thank you, God. I'm alive and well. I'm happy and grateful," and, "I'm strong. I'm happy. I'm wealthy." Then, I do two minutes of visualization.

I visualize my beautiful life and the beautiful things that I want. I want to see my kids happy and healthy, my business increasing, my book on shelves. I want to be fully inspired, growing, and knowledgeable.

After these exercises, I get up and drink a glass of room temperature water, brush my teeth, comb my hair, make coffee, and prepare to inspire myself. Then I'll read five or ten pages of a book or watch a short video from my personal coach. I might look up quotes on leadership. Sometimes I just think about a subject that I want to serve as inspiration for the day—leadership, growth, happiness, fitness, or success.

Because I believe the human brain is the most powerful computer in the universe, I'm always programming it, conditioning it to think the right way and go in the right direction. Affirmation, visualization, and inspiration serve as that programming early in the morning.

Inspiring Others

Next, I write because I want to further inspire my own journey and because I have committed myself to inspiring the people I love, including my family, friends, and the people I coach. I write messages about things I believe in to solidify my affirmations.

Mindset and Body Breaks

Before I move into my calls, I take a break to condition my body. I used to go to the gym every morning. For more than ten years, I went to the gym at 5:45 a.m. Now, I go in at 5:30 p.m. I also do some stretching every morning no matter what. After these rituals, I prepare my breakfast.

In the afternoon, I have a mindset break. I think everyone should have that in their day. No matter who you are or what you do, you are a human being and a bucket of energy; you get depleted throughout the day. When you build your schedule, plan to stop in the middle of the day for a quick ten minutes to replenish your energy.

These breaks help to realign your focus on what you want, and this time keeps you looking ahead at possibilities and opportunities. Then you will be reenergized to take action, rinse, and repeat!

Before the Energy Skill Can Become Ingrained

Before the energy skill is ingrained, throughout your daily plan of action, **awareness should be at the forefront** of your mind. You can't change, transform, improve, or even tweak your current energy and life if you don't even know what you need or what you're doing. You should be aware of everything.

Take time out of your day to check in with yourself and **recognize what negative thoughts and emotions,** like anger, fear, worry, doubts, panic, and sadness habitually enter your brain. Sometimes, we live in a pattern of low energy and don't even recognize it. Emotions are a habit. We get used to a pattern of emotions and it eventually becomes the norm. Usually, negative emotions and thoughts take energy away from us, just the same as negative people can.

The price of giving is receiving. Energy vibrates and ripples, and what you send into the universe will come back multiplied—1,000 times. If you're good at giving love, hope, gratitude, compassion, and optimism, those good things will come back to you. Likewise, the price of receiving is giving. If you tell the universe to "give me this and that," the universe will ask you to give in return. The more you want, the more it takes in kind.

When clients finish calls with me, they often tell me they feel more energy. They say, "Coach, when I finish my calls with you, I feel like I can conquer the world." It's the biggest compliment a coach—or parent, sibling, or friend—can get. I get goosebumps when I hear it! You can absolutely give energy, and people can receive and absorb it. But, you cannot give what you do not have.

When we spot a negative environment that depletes our energy and keeps us from giving, we have to move away from it as fast as we can. You can only control yourself, not the environment, so if it's at all possible, run. If you cannot get away from that negative environment, you have to work five times as hard to protect your mind space. You have to focus on the good you have in order to prevent contaminating yourself by absorbing and holding the negative. After all, **you can only give what you have and have what you give.**

Think of it like a force field. **Put yourself in a state of mind that creates strength again** and raise up a protective barrier to avoid absorbing the negative. Focus on good things, **affirm, decide, and act,** and work on controlling your thoughts and your emotions until you can get out of that environment and cleanse the negativity away. It is so important, because if you have negative energy, you can't give positive energy to others or to the universe.

Learn from Experience

Whatever negativity you are stuck with—whatever is depleting you that you have to overcome—can then become a learning experience. Every experience is a lesson. Always. There's so much truth in the saying, "What doesn't kill you makes you stronger." It expands your capabilities, taking you out of your normal zone as you experience different emotions and face new things. If you learn from them, breakdowns can lead to breakthroughs.

When a setback happens, ask yourself some questions to find the lesson. Write down the answers and get the situation out of your head and off your shoulders.

- Was it out of your control?
- Did you do your best?
- What did you learn from it?

These are important questions to ask, but don't stop here. Go further.

- What's funny about it?
- What am I going to do differently now so it doesn't happen again?

The Energy of Humor

People take life way too seriously! When we live too seriously, we become inflexible. That takes the fun out of life and makes it harder to enjoy your day-to-day life and routine.

I'm not saying you should loosen up so much that you stop taking care of the important people and things in your life. I'm saying we can be efficient, effective, focused, successful, and intense while still having fun as we go. Humor is such an important part of a balanced life.

Some of the biggest blockbuster movies and most popular TV shows are comedies. Famous comedians are highly paid because they bring humor to the lives of others. In Brazil, some of the most famous soap operas are ones that infuse humor in their acting.

Why? Because we feel wonderful when we laugh! We forget our problems for a while, and humor increases our energy and the feeling of well-being.

Just like everything else in life, it takes practice to use humor on a regular basis in our lives. Some people can do it more often and more effortlessly because they were exposed to humor growing up. Some weren't but made the decision to use it to get over the hurdles in life.

Humor is a wonderful habit because it makes us more flexible and willing to see the funny side of things, which will give us more clarity and focus. How? When we are open and not uptight, our thoughts and energy will flow better. We will be relaxed enough to see all the possible solutions more clearly and be able to make better decisions.

Laughter heals. We need to see the humor in situations because laughter rebuilds us. It allows us to release the feelings tied to the situation, letting the baggage go so it cannot linger and weigh us down. Find the humor and allow yourself to laugh about it. Then decide how to move forward. Let it go and refocus.

I realized the power of humor when learning from a tedious situation—I was eighteen years old and without a car. I was so busy doing so many things (and I was just beginning to make any money) so I didn't even think about buying one. Instead, I took the bus to go to university. Sometimes, the bus would take half an hour to come, on top of the fifty-minute ride to the school. Waiting in the sun, part of me would be so annoyed with it all. But, the other part, the part that yearned to learn, would remind me that this tedious situation was teaching me a skill. I was learning humor and patience.

That time, during which I could practice humor and patience, helped me improve and move toward living the life I wanted.

What You Believe Is What You Become

My grandmother, Noemia, believed that the words we speak impact our reality. Speak only of health and vitality and you will live a long, painless life. Speak of strength and be strong. On the other hand, speak of illness and be sick. She got this life lesson from following *Seicho-no-ie*, a Japanese philosophy created by Masaharu Taniguchi. This way of thought fascinated me. So, when I was eleven, my grandmother and my lovely aunt Solange took me to a *Seicho-no-ie* meeting.

At the time, my grandmother was about seventy years old with a seventeen-year-old's mindset. She was a musician and music teacher, very open-minded and progressive. And I was eleven going on seventeen, mature, observant, and I took everything in like a sponge.

During the meeting, a man spoke to the group about the philosophy and principles of Masaharu Taniguchi. I followed along in a booklet as he taught, then people came up and shared testimonials. One testimonial impacted me so much that I still remember it to this day.

A woman came forward and shared her story: "I was having a problem communicating with my husband. We were fighting and arguing. After remembering what Seich-no-ie has taught me, I decided to change my perception. Instead of looking at his imperfections and all the things I didn't like about him, I started visualizing, meditating, and focusing on the great things—how good a husband he is, how much he provides for me. Then I started writing little notes and leaving them all over the house. *Honey, I*

love you. You're a wonderful man. You're a wonderful father.
Then, I started to compliment him on the things he did
not yet do. *I love it when you help me in the kitchen.* I did
that because I remembered what Masaharu would say,
'Your words will reflect your mind, and that will become
your reality.'"

Even though her husband was a little dry, short-tempered,
and unhelpful, she changed the way she looked at him,
and that changed the way she interacted with him. Masaharu Taniguchi says that God is perfect, and we are the
sons and daughters of God, made in the image of God.
We are also perfect. The imperfections are external and
only come about from the things we tell ourselves—we
end up polluting our minds. At eleven years old, I inter-
nalized this mindset. What you say is what you become;
what you believe is what you become.

Notes to Myself

*What you say is what you become. What you believe is what
you become.* From that day on, I promised myself I would
be careful with what I said, because my mind was always
listening. I went a step further and started writing down
everything I wanted right then and there so I would be
conscious of what I said. I plastered my dreams and affirmations all over the walls of my bedroom. I wrote, "From
now on, I'm only going to speak positively." If someone

asked, "How are you?" I would tell them I felt "Great!" no matter what. I made the decision, wrote it down, and followed through. I spoke as many positive statements as possible. I worked until my enthusiasm was ingrained.

I also wrote, "I want to be rich," though, over time, I realized that what I wanted was to be financially independent. My mother was struggling with five kids and a separation. She had been a housewife with no real skills for employment. I watched her struggle and decided that I would never depend on anyone; neither my parents nor a spouse. Instead of just rich, my mission became more specific. "I'm going to learn, become very good at what I do, and make money. By the time I'm forty, I will be completely financially independent. That will mean I'm rich."

My grandmother and my Aunt Solange gave me the books on Masaharu Taniguchi, and I read other books as well. My life became better because I knew what I wanted, I paid attention to my mental programming, and I followed steps to make it happen. I believed the theory, and it became my reality.

Since that time, I have become a firm believer in the importance of reprogramming your mindset in order to achieve great success in all areas of your life. If you have a low-energy mindset, you will have low energy. Change your energy to a high-energy mindset, and see how far that can take you!

CHAPTER 3

Contagious Energy

—

*"People are about as happy as they
make their minds up to be."*

—ABRAHAM LINCOLN

Energy affects everyone around you. During the summer
of the year I turned seventeen, I met two girls from the
very south of Brazil. There was something about them
that was so intriguing.

They weren't particularly attractive, but they were so
charismatic and charming that they drew everyone to
them. I started to pay attention to try to figure out what
was so alluring about them. Their attraction, I found, was
simply that they smiled...all the time. I had already been
working on making smiling a habit, but that interaction
reinforced my decision even more, and I kept smiling as
an intentional exercise. People want to be around people

who radiate good energy, and smiling is one of the best ways to do that!

So, I taught myself to smile all the time. Smiling drew people in to me. I owe a lot of my professional success to that one simple skill!

Once, I tried to test the way that smiling affects people around me by being reserved and serious for an hour. Time stood still, and I couldn't keep up the veneer.

I failed the test because I simply could not break the habit of smiling!

Energy Is Infectious

Positive and negative energy surrounds us. Positive and negative energy waves vibrate at different frequencies. Faster, more intense vibrations are the "feel good," positive energy. While the slower, weaker vibrations are of the "feel bad" and negative variety. These vibrations are similar to those put out by radio waves; we can't see them, but we still know they exist. Whatever type of vibrations you put out will attract similar vibrations from others around you. So, if you put out fast, intense vibrations, you will connect with people on a similarly fast and intense wavelength.

We subconsciously and consciously communicate all the time through the energy vibrations we put out. We can feel when someone is putting out low energy, and we can also feel when someone is putting out high energy.

The Power of High Energy

From the ages of nineteen to twenty-one, I owned a bar in Brazil. I went to business school from 1:00 p.m. to 5:30 p.m., and I opened the bar from 6:00 p.m. to 2:00 a.m. every day—5:00 a.m. on the weekends. It was tough, but I've always worked hard.

I had ten waiters, seven employees, sixty-five tables, and two full bars to manage. It was a lot to track! But, I didn't just manage. I went above and beyond. I would walk around and talk to everybody, asking them how they were and what they needed. I was the owner, the host, and the love!

I rarely took time off, but on the rare occasion when I did, I always came back and heard the same comment, "Where were you? The energy just wasn't good without you in here!" My high energy pervaded throughout the bar, and apparently, it was so strong that my guests felt its absence.

Keeping Energy

My energy is my force field. It protects me and because of it, great stuff happens to me.

One time, I went to meet my son and his girlfriend for dinner. We met at a busy restaurant and parking is always impossible to find. It took my son and his girlfriend a half an hour to find a spot. My son's girlfriend turned to my son and said, "You just watch. You know your mom. She will pull right in, and get a spot very close to the restaurant." Sure enough, as I pulled up, a man backed out of a spot right in front of the restaurant and I pulled right in. When we got inside, they asked me about parking and I told them that it was a breeze! She turned to my son and said, "It's the bubble you told me about!" We shared a good laugh about it. My son continues to call my energy a "bubble."

Dealing with Negative People

Part of preserving the force field means I have to avoid the weak, slow, and toxic energy of negative people.

Negative energy is contagious, and so I try to avoid toxic people with negative energy.

I once had a client come from out of town to look at houses to buy. He was a toxic person, and I wanted to stop our business right from the beginning. But, I was still trying to please everybody, and I wanted a chance to work on my diplomacy skills. So, even though it didn't feel right to allow him to treat me so rudely—with his constant interrupting and his patronizing tone—I kept his business after the first meeting.

But, at the second meeting, he was still obnoxious, condescending, and mean. I decided I didn't have to accept the way he treated me or my business. I knew I couldn't try to convert him as a sale, so I decided to end our business that very day.

The time I spent trying to deal with him took the time of two or three healthy clients. He drained my emotions every time I saw him—my smile faded. So, I set a new rule. I will fire any client who takes my smile for an hour or more.

That client was an abusive complainer and a jerk—the markings of a very toxic person. Unfortunately, it is hard to avoid these types of people or situations, even for those of us who are very skilled at protecting our high energy. But, 10 to 15 percent of the time, some situations are just simply out of your control. If you find yourself in a situation where you are forced to interact with a person like this, take advantage of the 85 to 90 percent of what you can control and make sure to give yourself an "energy check-up and tune-up" afterward.

Remind yourself that you are allowed to have negative

feelings after dealing with negative people or events... you're human! But, you have to immediately work to replace your negative feelings with power or humor. Meditate or visualize happy things, repeat affirmations, listen to uplifting music, call a positive friend, watch a movie, read an inspiring book, list ten things for which you are grateful, read or tell a joke, plan something nice like a vacation, or get moving; do *anything* to rejuvenate yourself after dealing with those types!

Sharing Happiness

The billion-dollar question is: Can you convert people to be high-energy, happy people, or will some people always be negative and low energy?

Everything is possible. Every skill is learnable. I truly believe that. But happiness is an emotion, not an action. You can act happy, but without the actual emotion behind your action, it is empty. You've got to cultivate the mindset skill of making happiness a pattern. Like consistency and optimism, you must build it like a habit.

Everyone wants to be happy, and they can create a plan and develop rituals that will give them access to happiness.

But many people don't want to do the hard work of finding tools and creating rituals to get there. Instead, they wait for happiness to appear before them. Others don't even know happiness takes work. They believe it comes from the outside, that they'll be happy when their job is better or when they have more money or when they lose weight. They outsource their happiness, thinking it is a circumstance or a moment in time.

But, happiness is not external. Happiness is an emotion we can have with or without money. I've met a fisherman on the beach in Brazil who had next to nothing, only a boat and a hut. But, he had such a great attitude and energy of joy.

We need to give ourselves permission to find happiness first—before we retire, the kids are out of the house, or we have the money and the things we think will bring happiness. We can build a habit of happiness right now by focusing on the right things.

To the Moon

"Well, it's easy for you to be so happy...look at all you have!" My sister said this to me all the time.

One day, she called me and told me she was dealing with some difficulties. She admitted to me that she was feeling fearful. She said her life was going really well, so she felt like something bad was bound to be around the corner.

She told me, "It's so easy for you, though, Vanda, you were born with the *boom boom to the moon*." This is an expression in Brazil that means you're born with a burst of luck—you're a blast, all the way to the moon. She said, "You went to America, met a great guy, got married, and you have all these great things."

I told her, "Listen, darling, I might be fortunate, but I'm not lucky. I worked my ass off." Life is a constant grind. I've had professional failures; I've been lost. But, the difference is that I believe my fortune can come back and I took action to get what I wanted. I never stopped working, never stopped getting better. That great guy couldn't guide me to the things I wanted, and I could blow all that success to hell without the right work ethics and attitude. Nobody gives me anything or makes me do anything. I'm always asking myself what I need to do, who I need to meet, and what I need to learn.

"In life," I told her, "we don't get what we want or what we deserve. We get what we earn. I put in my time—I pay my dues, I study every moment, I work my ass off. Yes, I grew and got better, but I earned every bit of it."

She got offended, and maybe you are too, reading this.

I'm not saying you don't deserve these things. I'm saying God and the universe rewards in direct proportion to what you give. The more you work, the more you invest in yourself, the more you take the time to work on yourself and help other people, the more it comes back. My success is not because I was born lucky. It's due to the fact that I never stop working.

So, let's help you, now. Stop thinking about the things you don't have. Stop letting setbacks and breakdowns define you. When these things happen, you have to mourn to release the bad energy. Only then can you move on to regroup and refocus. There is a process, but most people prefer to remain a victim of circumstance.

My sister went on to break out of the rut and do much better. Will you?

Easy Is as Easy Does

When someone comments about things being easy for me, I usually ask them to tell me what they mean by that. Often, they don't know how to clarify their response. What came easy for me? I came to America with $500 in my pocket, no savings, and only able to speak a couple words in English. What was easy about that?

It wasn't really easy at all—but if I can do it, you can do it.

It's not easy, but it can be simple. Not long ago, I told

one of my clients, "There are no secrets." You can find anything you want to know in books or online; the secret is out, but just because everyone has access to it, doesn't mean they will take advantage of it.

Studies have shown that only 10 percent of people put what they learn into action.

The map to success is there, but the real question is whether you will follow it and for how long.

Bad things have happened to me, as they will for everyone. But I practice what I teach. I believe in creating a plan and following it. I'm not an analytical person, but I do believe in systems, methods, and a step-by-step action plan. I played basketball as a teenager, and there was always a coach to help me. My coaches told me the plays, where to go and what to do, so I followed them. Their direction led me to success. I still follow the advice of business coaches to this day.

Yes, these plans will get us to where we want to be, but we also need to learn how to overcome obstacles and setbacks that we encounter along this journey.

Coping with Tragedy

We are human beings. Tragedy is inevitable. Pain happens,

but we don't need to live in suffering! We have to accept that fact and deal with its reality. We cannot sweep it under the rug. We cannot hide it. We cannot lock it deep inside; it will fester. It will make us sick, and it will physically present itself in the form of high blood pressure, ulcers, insomnia, and pain.

That's why I keep myself coachable, so I can follow plans to recover.

Mourn your tragedies. Feel the upset and sit with the rejections and setbacks. Allow the anger to come and go. Don't just let them take over, but control the emotions. Give yourself time to mourn and feel. Then, when you have allowed it to come, refocus and let it go. In the case of tragedy, I refocus on celebrating the person as they were.

About three years ago, on July 15, my mom died from a stroke. A month and a half later, I was still mourning for my mom when I got another heartbreaking call. I was told that my beautiful sister, Vanja, was being flown to the mainland from her home for treatment for an aneurysm. She was in a coma for ten days, underwent surgery, had another stroke, and then died. She was only in her fifties. We were so close, and it was a very difficult time for me. I was in shock.

Meanwhile, in those days, I was carrying forty-eight clients. I had to compartmentalize my feelings during the day, because I had to be on the phone for six to eight hours. Once my day ended, I would cry for the rest of the night and start again the next day. It was one of the most difficult times in my life.

Throughout those early days and beyond, I practiced what I teach. I practiced positivity even during my lowest time. In many ways, the positive energy I had to create to share with my clients saved me. I focused on my clients, giving them love, attention, and coaching. I wasn't resentful that I had to work. Instead, I was grateful I could work to get out of my grief for a bit. Helping my clients healed me. They never even knew what was happening.

I'm not claiming that I didn't feel pain. I did. I felt a lot of it. But, I told myself I needed to let it go. I needed to let it pass. Then, I made the decision that I would celebrate my sister and mother. I would celebrate my mother for her amazing, funny, exciting, and enthusiastic self. I would celebrate my sister and her love of cooking by learning how to cook. I realized I had no other option but to honor their lives by being the person they wanted me to be.

Strength in Vulnerability

This time in my life was certainly a test, and, at many points along the way, I felt like I learned a lot of lessons and I grew a lot. I have no doubt that I am a strong person and can learn the things I need to and do the things I must. But for the first time in my life, I felt vulnerable. I could die tomorrow. I wasn't superwoman.

Instead of collapsing, I continued to follow through with my plans, but now with a renewed sense of urgency. I had to enjoy more, be more, and do more for other people. I couldn't feel guilty or regret anything. I had to be careful to filter my environment, my thoughts, and my energy. I had to walk on the beach and do things for myself. I was no longer living just for me, but for my mom and my sister as well. Moving forward in vulnerability added to my strength rather than draining it.

That time in my life presented major hurdles for me in my journey. But, I overcame them and in a way, they made me stronger. My resolve to get where I wanted to be only increased.

The Energy of Time

While waiting in the Sacramento airport for a flight to Palm Springs, I met an older gentleman. He was in his early nineties and we got into a conversation, as I often do. My niece is always asking me if I have to talk to *everybody*. I have a friendly face, and I love people. What can I say?

The older man and I were chatting about the trip, and he was going to play golf in spite of his age. I thought it was fantastic that he was still in good shape, so I asked him, "What's the key to a beautiful, healthy life like yours?" He told me what my father-in-law, Peter, used to tell me all the time.

He said, "I eat meat, I drink wine, but everything is in moderation. Not too much, not too radical. Moderation is the key."

We grieve in moderation. Not too much, not too radical. We allow it, and we move on.

Contagious Energy Recharges Us

The godmother of my youngest son is one of my best friends. She's like a sister from a different mother, my *comadre*, as we say. She's also a tough businesswoman and owns multiple companies—at one point, she owned up to six! She's a very smart woman and quite knowledgeable. We have coaches for business, but we also need friends like this who we can turn to. I count on Giselle as that person. I can always turn to her and say, "Hey, got a minute? Let me pick your brain."

People who spend time with their friends—especially friends like Giselle—are healthier than those who spend their time alone or are constantly too busy to connect.

When you are out with your best friends, the people you love, your partner, or your kids, you have an opportunity to laugh and smile. All that love and joy heals, empowers, and strengthens you. It fills you up and recharges you, just like a battery.

Love, joy, and connection are strong, clean, and powerful emotions. They are healing. Whenever you feel love and joy, your energy is at its highest level. Go out, connect, love, and enjoy!

SECTION II

Energy in Action

CHAPTER 4

Clear Energy

———

"The things that matter most must never be at the mercy of the things that matter least."
—ARISTOTLE

I coach from what I have learned, studied, experienced, and observed. Mostly importantly, I coach from my beliefs.

One thing I strongly believe is that clarity is king. My girlfriends would correct me and say, "Clarity is queen." That's good, too. The point is, clarity is everything.

If you don't know exactly what you want and why you want it, how will you get anywhere? Without a clear destination and plan, you might leave New York and wind up in Mexico! You could set sail to Europe but wind up in Africa! Clarity is everything. We've got to know what we want and why we want it if we expect to get anywhere on our journey.

Clarity is fundamental. I have to reiterate this over and over to myself, my kids, and my clients. My clients come to me hungry for direction, so I coach them in order to establish clarity of their goals and to help them plan their roadmap to success.

Knowing Specifically What You Want Raises Your Energy

I have a friend who took a severance package to open a beauty salon. However, she didn't have clarity about her outcome, specific goals, the right business skills, resources, or the right people to help. Because of that, she wasn't successful, and she ran out of money before the place even opened. It was very sad because she sunk all her savings into the venture.

Unfortunately, this is not a rare story. This type of failure happens every day. I see it all the time. If you are vague in your goals, you won't have enough information to make anything happen. If you tell me you want to be happy, well, great. To me, that could mean something completely different than it does to you. What do you mean by "happy?" My coach told me that when you are vague, you have pain, but when you have clarity, you can make things happen.

Priority Number 1: Clarity

Many times, people don't get what they want because they don't even know what they want in the first place. They don't know what to focus on, so they can't grow and expand in the right way. In fact, I have read that only 3 percent of the population have any sort of defined goals at all!

"I want to be financially independent." Okay, what does that look like? "I want to be powerful." Great! What does "power" mean to you?

You have to know what you want to work toward and achieve. When a client asks how to find clarity in their life, I ask them to open up and tell me about their life. Together, we explore what motivates them, what pressures they have, where they came from, and how they view themselves. We talk about what they love, what they like to do, and what they'd like to see. We drill down to the specifics.

I ask questions like, "If you could do anything you wanted right now, what would it be? What do you truly want? Where do you see yourself? What makes you feel joy and enthusiasm? What are you passionate about? What are your dreams? When was the last time you took an hour to think about your dreams? Are you thinking about thriving or just surviving?"

Dreams Add Clarity

My mom left my dad when I was ten. My father was a great guy, but he was difficult to live with. After my mom and us kids left, we wound up moving a lot. In some ways, in those days, starting over made me feel perpetually "unsettled." I always had new friends, new schools, and new cities to learn, over and over. Books were my escape. I could sit down with a good fantasy book and slip into another world. In that world, I felt stable and safe; it was my sanctuary during difficult times. It raised my energy and helped me feel good in spite of living a transient life.

I spent a lot of my childhood honing the ability to daydream, or dream while awake. During those dreams, I dreamed up my ideal life. I envisioned myself traveling, happy, healthy, and rich. At that time, I didn't know what visualization was, but that is exactly what I was doing. My visualizations helped me create a clear picture of my life as I wanted it to be. They also allowed me the freedom to dream as big, fun, and colorful as I wanted. I never put restraints on myself. I never questioned if what I was dreaming could happen. My life could be anything I wanted! That helped me to have clear and big goals. To me, it was only a question of time whether they would come true.

Later, when I was going to university, I carried these dreams with me and would tell people about them. When

I say I'm going to do something, I do it. Not everyone believes me, of course, because not everyone thinks big. I talked about going to Europe—never really thinking about America—and I visualized it happening. Though my reality veered slightly from this, I used the visualization to think bigger, believing in a better future, a better time, a better me. Those dreams gave me the clarity I needed to make it happen.

Priority Number 2: Know Why You Want It

Some days, you won't feel like working on any of this. Without a clear and passionate purpose, you have nothing to leverage. But, with a strong *why* you can put a map together to follow and take action.

Let's say that financial fulfillment for one of my clients means they can afford their dream car. First, I ask them *why* they want the car. That *why* has to be very specific and concise. The *why* is the leverage that inspires and motivates you to keep going.

Visualization and the Why

I teach my clients to use visualization to understand what they want in order to understand their *why*. From there, once they have a clear view on the *why* through visualization, they can then find the willpower to motivate themselves to make changes to get where their visualizations take them.

Priority Number 3: The Game Plan
Put Your Goal Up and Visualize It on a Scoreboard

Once we figure out exactly what we want and why we want it, we can work to achieve it through a goal scoreboard.

In order to help my clients set a plan and track their progress, I ask them to make a scoreboard.

On that scoreboard, I have them break down what they need to accomplish to get the car. "What do you need to do, Monday through Friday, for a few hours a day, to get the car? What are your 'musts?' What appointments do you have to make? What leads do you have to follow? What profits do you have to attain?" Because we know there will be days you don't feel like doing these things, you also need accountability. "Who can you talk to every day who can remind you to keep working? Between the board, your visualization, and your accountability, can you make this happen? Will it motivate you to get it done in time—maybe by December 15 as a Christmas present to yourself?"

You will need to inspire yourself every day. It's hard at first, but like everything else, it is a muscle and it will get easier over time. To do this, it is important to get in the right mindset. It is how we think and perceive life. Discipline, resilience, consistency, and commitment all lead to the proper mindset to execute with.

Scoreboard in Action

I speak three languages. But, years ago, I did not have that skillset.

During my teenage years after my parents separated, I did a lot of traveling back and forth from one parent to the other. When I was sixteen, I took the bus from Sao Luis to Bahia to visit my father. It takes about two and a half days on the bus to go from one state to another, so my journey was long.

Bahia is one of the top tourist destinations in Brazil, so while I was on the bus, I met a man who was there visiting. I smiled at him, and he said something I didn't understand. So, he tried again in another language, and I still didn't understand. He tried three different languages that I couldn't follow at all. When he finally tried Spanish, we were able to communicate a little. But the damage was done.

I felt so ignorant. Here I was, sixteen years old, living in a country rampant with tourists, and I only spoke one language. Meanwhile, this guy could speak three or four and I couldn't even talk to him! I told myself then that by the year 2000 I would be able to speak four languages. That was my goal. So, I set a scoreboard in motion. I partitioned out how long I thought it would take to learn each language, and I went out and signed up for language classes as soon as I could.

Now, I speak three languages. I was able to accomplish that through hard work, of course, but also because I had a very clear idea of what I wanted. I wanted to speak four languages by the year 2000, and I had a scoreboard to check my progress.

Apply This Thinking to Your Business

You can apply my simple methodology to your business objectives. For me, I broke down my goal of learning four languages into doable chunks. I didn't try to learn them all at once. I paced myself and planned.

For your business objective, determine the path you need to take and break down the path into segments; then, put them on a scoreboard. For instance, if it is your goal to get to $500,000 in sales in the next year, determine how many sales that will take. Determine how many clients you will need to get that many sales. Then, go a step deeper and determine how many calls you will need to make to get that many clients.

Track your progress on your scoreboard!

Dream Board

I also recommend making a dream board for your goals. Don't confuse a scoreboard with a dream board. A dream board should be filled with all your *whys*, all your wants, and all your dreams. The scoreboard holds the numbers, the actions that it takes to get to specific parts of your dream. The scoreboard makes the dream board a reality.

This process will lead you to the success you seek.

CHAPTER 5

Success with Energy

"All breaks you need in life wait within your imagination; imagination is the workshop of your mind, capable of turning mind energy into accomplishment and wealth."

—NAPOLEON HILL

I observe successful people because I want to learn from them. I am a lifelong learner, as are most successful people. We always want to be learning because we know that is the secret to growing and improving.

To be a learner, you have to be teachable or coachable. You have to follow the clues and directions that others have left for you. Sure, you could push your way into some form of success by banging your head against the wall, but most people understand there are better ways to get what you want. Instead of trying repeatedly to no avail, successful people look to the people who have already made it. They observe these people, learn from them, and follow the path already forged.

Learning from Others

Masaharu Taniguchi said, "The wise one learns from someone else's experience."

We don't have to suffer through an experience to learn a lesson. We don't have to feel the pain ourselves. We can learn from what others have already lived. This principle has guided my mission to search for people who are successful, observe others who have struggled, and learn from them.

The more you learn and reinforce what you've learned, the more you can do and the more you will want to do. The momentum of those actions will compound. Instead of taking little steps, you'll make big leaps.

Optimism

In all my years studying successful people, I have found that the number one quality most of them share is unrelenting optimism. They have a positive state of mind, which enhances their outlook on life.

This optimism allows them to have many other fabulous qualities. They are highly energetic, which allows them to do more than the average person. They seem to have more fun. Their vibrant energy makes those around them feel good.

Lastly, they smile—a lot!

Smiling is attractive and contagious; we are drawn to people who smile. I've observed this for decades in my own life and in the lives of other successful people. But it goes deeper than that. Dr. Robert Zagone's research tells us that smiling creates a physiological change that makes you feel better. A smile truly does send messages to your brain, chemically and physically. It tells your brain you should feel good.

Passion

I've also observed that successful people are passionate. Passion is linked to clarity. When you know what you are passionate about, what makes you happy, you will feel better and be more successful. Passionate people know exactly what makes their heart warm. When you find what you love and make that your life, nothing will feel like work. That passion will charge your energy battery so you're inspired, motivated, and operating at the highest levels. It creates a perfect storm of energy, joy, and fulfillment. That kind of energy is contagious.

When you find that sweet spot of passion, your energy shows on your face, vibrating out toward everyone around you. People will be drawn to you like a magnet, wanting more of what you have, both in business and in life.

This speaks to the Law of Attraction: what you put out comes back to you.

I Applied These Lessons

I applied these lessons to my life. The more I studied, learned, and read, the better I felt. The more I exercised, the more I could do.

Conviction and commitment in all areas of my life hardened. I was able to involve myself in many pursuits and projects at once. These activities created energy, and that energy created more energy. Suddenly, I was able to do more and be more than I ever thought possible. This drove my passion, which in turn propelled my conviction.

This conviction comes out when I interact with people, and my energy and enthusiasm allow me to inspire and motivate others.

I am unstoppable.

Energy of Resilience

During the four years of my business administration degree, I took classes in São Luis, Ma. Brazil. Our building was located right next to the veterinary school. The campus layout was open, and we could see the veterinary school's fenced area for horses and goats.

One goat would try to break into the other side of the enclosure. He'd push and push at the fence, occasionally breaking through. No matter how often people came out to close the fence and keep him out, he'd keep trying. He was a resilient old goat.

As I went on with my studies, I started to notice those moments of resilience in my own life. I could feel that stubbornness—in a good way!—and would envision myself as the resilient goat. I keep moving toward the results that I believe in, no matter what. Whatever rejections, setbacks, challenges, or breakdowns come my way, I will keep on going to the end.

I call it Goat Syndrome. My sons are not fond of this term, but I love it! Goat Syndrome will help you stand up after getting knocked down a thousand times when you're doing something for your family, your goals, your dreams. When you are resilient like an old goat, it won't matter what obstacles get in your way. You will keep trying as many times as it takes to get the job done.

There are goats that live at the very tops of snowy, rocky mountains where few other animals can survive. Their natural resilience and strength, with a good dose of cleverness, makes it work. Goat Syndrome is an attitude that keeps you in the game, no matter how often you fall or fail.

Resilience and persistence are two of the most important skills for anyone to develop, especially if you are in business. You are going to make mistakes. You are going to fail. Not one person's life has been perfect, so you have to figure out how to take the punch and shake it off to keep moving. Underneath these skills, you will find mental strength, determination, emotional strength, and consistency. As you cultivate each of those traits, resilience and persistence will become part of your nature. You will develop Goat Syndrome.

Putting Energy into Action

A client of mine was having trouble building energy in his daily routine. He felt stuck and uninspired in his daily life. This happens often, actually. People tell me they don't feel excited about anything. They have no desire to do more and don't know how to break out of that funk. Even when they make good money and have a nice house, or the things people think bring happiness and energy, people get stuck. Happiness is an emotion that comes with growth and progress, so when you aren't growing, you feel unhappy.

With this client, our goal was to find what made him happy, excited, and passionate again. We also needed a good reward for the effort that would involve. So, we incentivized him with a vacation that he would take three months out. To prepare for his vacation, he would need to accomplish goals at work. We set about creating a clear action plan for him. Each day, he had to accomplish three things by a certain time.

The top 3 percent of billionaires, champions, experts, and successful people wake up before six in the morning. But, this client woke up late every morning. In order to get him on track for success and in the top 3 percent, we had to make sure he got up early. We took steps to reorganize his day, including planning the night before to make sure he was ready to get out of bed at 5:30 a.m.

The challenge for me was not to tell him to wake up earlier, but to help him see the benefits and commit to the outcome. He had to believe that building his mindset, shaping his attitude, and creating great habits and rituals happens best in the morning. Build your business early in the day while you still have energy, while life is not so busy. When you get all the important, challenging things done by 10:30, you can say, "I got a job done," and you can move on with your life for the rest of the day.

This story shows us how we can plan for short-term goals, but this practice also works for planning in the long term. I have practiced this skill so much that I can effectively plan for years in advance.

Immediate Gratification

Reaching a goal is so difficult because it takes persistence and grit to keep doing something long enough to make it a habit. In order to see habit-building results, it takes ninety days of sustained effort. For many, that seems too far away. Some intense efforts that take several hours each day can provide quicker results, but not everyone can develop the level of consistency and persistence that this requires. People want immediate results and instant gratification. When the results take time, they start to doubt the process and themselves. Then, they quit.

Millennials are prone to this. They grew up with the internet, and thus, the need for immediate gratification. Millennials don't know how to live outside of a world where they can't get things at the click of a button.

Regardless, persistence and resilience are worth pursuing.

These are all skills that can be learned and improved. We just have to decide we want to.

Clarity Brings Success Close

I believe a lot of people cannot see the future clearly. So, we have to use visualization. The less we know what we want, the more difficult it is to see where to go. Visualization brings that image of our desired future closer to us. The clarity raises the energy we need to inspire and motivate us toward persistence and resilience.

A vague goal like "make a lot of money" is not really what you are looking for. You really want the feeling and experience that comes with it, don't you? You want the security of the income, or the ability to choose your child's school, and so on. These are the things you must visualize.

Let's say I have a client who is pursuing a goal of $500,000. That alone would not get him out of bed in the morning. He would need to visualize paying off his house, vacationing in Paris, and setting aside a college fund for his children. So, those three things would go on his dream board. Before getting out of bed, for two or three minutes, I would have him envision depositing that check into the college fund. I would have him picture himself on the Seine in Paris, and writing the last check to pay off his mortgage.

If your goal is to sell fifty homes, you've got to see yourself showing the house. You have to envision signing the contract and getting paid for the sale. You have to imagine yourself walking into the bank with a check in your hand. You have to picture yourself smiling at the bank teller as the money is deposited into your account. The image has to be clear. It has to be enticing so that your energy raises and the future is revealed. This is the kind of motivation that will get you out of bed and into the zone doing what your goals require, even when your energy is low.

Mastering Visualization

Follow these guidelines to become a master of visualization:

1. Imagine and dream to your fullest extent.
2. Be very clear and specific about the picture in your mind.
3. Use all your senses in the process: see, hear, smell, etc.
4. Visualize the results throughout the day.
5. Carry the picture in your mind.
6. Think, dream, talk, move, walk with confidence that what you want will happen.

Frustration Can't Be a Deal Breaker

Sometimes, especially in the beginning, there will be days when you just feel like you can't do it. Let's be honest, most days we all want to be sitting on the beach drinking a Mai Tai or zoned out on the couch reading a book. That's the *easy* way to do life. Working toward a goal, striving, and doing are harder. We must do it anyway. You have to pay your dues. When you find yourself frustrated with the process, return to your *why* board. Remind yourself why you are striving.

Next, embrace the frustration. It is how you grow. Remember, frustration is natural. It is not a deal breaker. It can and should be overcome. To deal with frustration, ask yourself why you are frustrated. What part of the process has you feeling down? If it's taking too long, what part did you expect to move quicker? After you dig to the heart of your frustration, you can create a plan to take action and keep moving forward.

Let's look at it in a real-life example. If I'm going to lose ten pounds in two months, I can plan to lose one or two pounds each week. So, I set my daily calorie limit and determine how many calories I need to burn. That translates into a specific workout and a meal plan.

Then, dig deeper again. Are you taking the right amount of action in consistent ways? If I start to falter in any of those steps—1,400 calories instead of 1,100, or 200 burned instead of 300—the results aren't going to come as quickly as I'd planned. Before I turn my frustration into despair and quit, I look at why the results are slow to come. Maybe I need another thirty days. Maybe I need to be more consistent or pursue it with more intensity. Maybe I need to work out six days each week instead of five. In any case, if I am not following the formula, I cannot expect results.

For results to show up, you have to be consistent. Momentum builds when you do the same actions every day. Wishing for a goal will not make it happen. Doing a few of the tasks will not get you there, either.

Visualize yourself at the finish line and set a plan to get there. Your daily schedule, which is the topic of the next chapter, is the map to the diamonds (aka your goals). Find your diamonds, then pursue them with intensity and consistency, all the while being persistent in the face of setbacks and obstacles.

In the end, setbacks, especially the small ones, make you stronger and better able to strive.

CHAPTER 6

Schedule Your Energy

——

"Life gets better when we get better."
—JIM ROHN

Your daily schedule is your map to the diamonds. Without one, you are just winging it.

Many people think they don't need a map. They say, "I'm open for anything!" This sounds like a poetic way to live but it's reactive. Without a map, who knows where you'll end up? A daily schedule takes you right where you want to go—right for the diamonds.

Your daily schedule is your GPS, telling you when you've gotten off course and when you are right on track. Use your daily schedule to reflect on your goals and remind yourself to keep pursuing them. Success in business is 80 percent of what you think about and what you focus on. Make sure that 80 percent is comprised of your goals.

Make Plans However You Can

Making a map should be easy. Google docs? Do you like to use planners, notebooks, or plain paper? Your map is your daily schedule, so choose something you will use every day. It must be simple and easy to follow through with.

My phone keeps me on track. I dictate calendar items to Siri, set alarms, and color code activities so I can quickly see what is happening. Everything goes on my calendar. Business, breaks, gym, rest, fun. I will even put beach time on my calendar! I put everything down in my planner because that gives me the freedom to not have to worry. As long as I follow my schedule, I know nothing is left out.

I know when to work, when to play, and when to rest.

I know when it's time to be Vanda the mother, Vanda the coach, Vanda the friend, and Vanda the partner.

I know exactly when I need to change my hat.

Too often, we avoid schedules and planners because we

think they are restrictive. I take a different view entirely. Without a written schedule to keep me on track, I feel lost.

How often do you find yourself still worried about work when you should be resting, or working so long that you never take a break to play? Or maybe you get caught up in playing and struggle to catch back up at work. When I schedule in work and play, I can fully commit to those moments. When it's time to play, I have no guilt. I can head down to the beach knowing I've done my work already. I can put my feet up and truly relax. Likewise, when I work, I don't mix play into it and get distracted. I know that time is coming.

To effectively plan your days, you will need to include the following in your daily schedule:

1. Morning routine with visualization, affirmation, exercise, and inspiration time
2. Meals and breaks
3. Moments to recondition, program, train, and inspire your brain
4. Joy, fun, and laughter
5. Steps or daily action toward your "must achieve" goals
6. Education time
7. Recharge time with your loved one and in nature
8. Exercise for energy, health, and disposition

Morning Rules the Day

If you don't protect your schedule in the morning, you won't get everything done.

The morning routine is sacred and immensely important. Your morning routine will make or break you. Get the most important things out of the way in the morning, before life happens. Every successful businessperson always does the most important things first. Success leaves clues. There is no reason to reinvent the wheel—emulate! Leaving important tasks for later diminishes the probability that you will do them to 30 percent. Willpower is finite: it is strongest in the morning and dwindles throughout the day. Even the most disciplined person in the world will get distracted! So, take advantage of your willpower before distractions come up, before drama flares, and before the rest of the world wakes up. Focus on your future until 10:30 a.m. When those things are out of the way, they are protected no matter what happens in the afternoon.

With the important things secured and out of the way, your energy levels will rise for the rest of the day. Getting the most important things done in the morning not only raises your productivity and profitability, but it also raises your energy, well-being, feeling, and enthusiasm. It feels great! You'll feel better knowing you've accomplished the big stuff already.

Getting through the morning helps you achieve what

Charles Duhigg describes as a "small win." Small wins help you experience a small sense of accomplishment. When some people say, "So what if you got through the morning, you still have the rest of the day to overcome!" I tell them that getting through the morning is a small victory that will give them the confidence and energy to overcome the next hurdle. If you can win in the morning, that winning feeling will carry you.

Several tips I have found helpful in my morning routine, include:

1. Don't look at your phone. Keep yourself centered and focused on the task at hand. Looking at your phone for emails and Facebook notifications will pull your attention away to shallower pursuits.
2. Do not schedule open or free time during the mornings. The lack of direction and sense of accomplishment that comes from "doing nothing" will only hinder your motivation for the rest of the day.
3. Remember, your calendar is a working document, which means you don't have to follow everything perfectly. Things come up, plans change, and you can reschedule accordingly. But make the morning routine solid.
4. Don't leave it for later. Many people have mastered the art of pushing things off. Don't make this a habit. Little things add up and become important, big things later.

Welcome to the World

We like to say, "Where has the time gone?" It feels like there aren't enough hours in the day, and we don't know where the time was wasted. We feel busy all day long but don't have much to show for it.

When clients tell me these things, I empathize. I tell them, "I appreciate your struggle here, and I understand. Welcome to the biggest struggle of the human race—time management."

Every single person struggles to manage their time. We have only twenty-four hours in a day, and when you work eight to ten hours of that time, it's difficult to know what to do (and not do) with the time you have.

Welcome to the world.

You can always get more money, but you cannot get more time. That's why we are in pursuit of energy. If you build your energy up and then know how to spend it, you can do more with those hours. You can get ahead of the game. When you can do more in less time, it's just as good as—if not better than—gaining more hours in a day.

You're not going to be able to do every single thing you'd like to do in a day. That's an empty dream, not a realistic pursuit. But, here is where the Pareto Principle comes into effect.

Twenty percent of your actions—decisions, tasks, activities—generates 80 percent of your business and momentum. Protect that 20 percent. Put those tasks on your daily schedule and follow them like a map. This will help you figure out what is important to accomplish in your allotted time. Then, you will be able to squeeze more out of your time.

Positive and Negative Affirmations

If you are like most people, you will have trouble keeping your brain engaged as you move through your daily schedule. You may get sucked into the dramas, fires, and hang-ups that we all encounter throughout the day. Bad thought habits like, "Why am I even doing this? I can't do this. I'm not good enough," leave you weighed down with negativity, and you end up putting yourself down. This deters you from completing your goals.

Instead, I tell myself at least three times each day that I am "super-efficient." My boys laugh when I say, "I have a great memory. I remember everything." Maybe I do, maybe I don't. It doesn't matter. What matters is that, like in software programming, I am telling my brain—the powerful computer that it is—how to operate. If I'm going to use the most powerful computer in the universe for my own best experience, I'm going to program it to perfection. I'm not going to let it run amuck. It's going to do exactly what I want it to do.

Brainwash yourself. *You are smart. You learn fast. You're efficient. Everything you do, you do very well. You can do anything you want.* Tell yourself these statements over and over, until you believe them.

Stay Accountable

I keep myself accountable to my schedule and use techniques (like the positive affirmations mentioned above) to keep myself going back to the schedule. I also visualize my goals and results multiple times per day.

When I started selling real estate, I used this technique. I told myself, "I list and sell one home a day. I list and sell one home a day." Twelve years later, I was selling one home every other day.

Another technique I use is to surround myself with people who care about me and support me. I enlist the help of a coach, a friend, or my family. I have two coaches—the CEO of our company, who is my great coach, and another great coach who helps me. They help me stay on track.

I also openly share my goals with people. Just saying my goals out loud makes me feel like I have to stay accountable and accomplish them, lest I look like a flake. The last thing I want is for my family to say, "Oh, here comes Vanda with another tall tale. She never goes through with it."

I also actively work to clean out my schedule for moments where I am wasting time. I audit myself, and you should to. Learn how you spend your time. Take a day and write out everything you did for every half hour. Notice which hours you are wasting time. Look for the triggers that make you waste time (like boredom, hunger, loneliness) and work to figure out new ways to stop those triggers from affecting your productivity.

I plan my schedules with a future in focus. To do that, I use reverse calculation to reach my goals. In order to explain reverse calculation, I will give you the example of how I worked toward my house in Tahoe.

I really wanted a vacation house in Tahoe, California. So, the first thing I did was I figured out how much it was going to cost me. Then, I calculated how many houses I would need to sell to earn the down payment. Then I figured out how much the mortgage was, and calculated how many houses I needed to sell per month in order to cover it. I worked out the details and decided I needed to sell an extra twelve homes in six months. That meant I needed to sell a house every two weeks. To do that, I knew from experience I needed three appointments per week. To make that happen, I needed to have fifteen conversations with potential clients per day.

Every day, I worked on those conversations while envisioning that vacation home and the lovely memories I would create there with my family. With the combination of reverse calculation and the power of a Daily Focus Mindset, it worked!

Daily Focus Mindset

I have a list of sample affirmations at the end of the book to help you on your journey to creating a great Daily Focus Mindset that will get you in the mood to achieve your daily goals. Visualize where you want to be, make a plan to get there, plan it out, and follow the schedule to get to the diamonds!

SECTION III

Body and Soul Energy

CHAPTER 7

Eat, Drink, and Breathe Energy

———

"The way to improve your life
is to improve yourself."
—BRIAN TRACY

I love rocking the boat and challenging myself to change my mindset.

Once, after I attended a Tony Robbins event, I quit coffee and milk for eleven months and beef, lamb, and pork for three and a half years. Tony spoke about how those things weighed down our energy and I wanted to challenge myself to see if it was true. He was right! Now, I drink coffee again because I enjoy it. But, I don't overdo it!

After that event, I also challenged myself to eat even more

vegetables. To motivate myself to do so, I reprogrammed my association with vegetables. I reminded myself that they will give me energy and prolong my health. Now, I eat a lot more vegetables!

This illustrates an important point: human beings have the ability to change and adapt to that change. This can be a good thing or a bad thing. For instance, we can adapt to living an overindulgent, hedonistic life. Or, we can adapt in a positive way, like eating things that are healthy for us but that we don't necessarily enjoy in the beginning. Adapting to get yourself to do good things increases your energy and improves your disposition.

This is important, because, as I learned from my mentor, Jim Rohn, all disciplines are connected. When you start to work on one thing, the ripples of that action affect others. When you take care of your body, your mind improves. Certain foods will literally feed your brain. Improving certain things in your life will improve all of it. Specific habits such as regular exercise and healthy eating that affect all your other habits are what Charless Duhigg calls "Keystone Habits." Keystone habits have a wide influence on other habits. For instance, a person who exercises will often perform better at work, eat better, and have healthier sleep patterns.

We are extremely adaptable beings, and that can be either

good or bad. You can adapt to eating well just as you adapted to eating poorly. You can adapt to being wealthy and you can adapt to being broke.

You might be thinking you can't do it. You can't enjoy those foods or exercise that much. But when you have the right discipline to enact change and adapt, when your *why* is big enough, you can do anything. And when it affects your energy, you must.

Move for Energy

The mind and body must be improved together. For that reason, fitness and nutrition are intricately tied to your success in improving your mindset and energy level. You cannot increase your energy if you are unhealthy. You need to balance your mental energy with your physical energy.

Exercise improves and strengthens your body. From that virtuous cycle, your energy levels improve.

Reprogram Your Assumptions

If healthy habits are new to you or you resist them, take another step back to look at the problem. What is your aversion? Do you think exercise is painful or difficult? Do you think it isn't good for you? Do you feel like you don't have time? Time management is the most common excuse I hear and my biggest pet peeve. When someone says they don't have enough time, I want to remind them who they are talking to.

None of us feel like we have the time. But if you really want it, you'll find it. You will make the time.

A helpful way to reprogram your brain is by realigning your associations. Associate your goals with pleasure rather than pain. It might seem like a complicated practice, but you already do it all the time.

Think about your romantic partner, for instance. If you are in a healthy relationship, you will associate him or her with love, happiness, and a warm feeling. When you see that person, all those feel-good feelings will bubble up. This is the same experience we have with food. Most people associate burgers, pasta, pizza, and sweets with happiness and abundance. They associate broccoli, carrots, and celery with restriction.

But, to start eating healthier, you can flip those associations. If you want to stop eating burgers and pizza, then associate them with diabetes, cancer, sickness, vomit, fever, and fat. Then sooner or later, that food will not be appetizing at all.

If you think of pain, sweat, and hard work when you think

about exercise, it won't be appealing. Instead, associate it with feeling good, having stamina and energy, breathing better, and looking better. Sooner or later, you're going to start enjoying it.

To be human is to be adaptable. If you do something enough and tell yourself that it is good for you enough, it will always become a habit. The story you tell yourself becomes your reality. You simply must decide what you'd rather adapt to.

Get That Rush

Let's say you want to get in shape. To begin your journey, you have to first create the right mindset around fitness. To do this, we can use the same strategy we use to attain any goal. We use clarity, visualization, reasons, and then action. First, have a clear vision of what you want to accomplish. Do you want to lose weight? Do you want to gain muscle? Do you want to run a faster mile? Do you want to make healthy choices like using stairs instead of elevators? Be very clear with your intentions.

Next, visualize what you will look like when you reach your goal. Will you weigh less? Will you have abs? Will your skin glow? Will you look better in your clothes? Personally, I like looking good. I bet you do too!

Next, take action. Write out a plan to do some form of

exercise four to six days a week and thirty to sixty minutes a day or more, depending on your plan. It is difficult to do at first, but after you follow through for a while and your habits appear, you'll be hooked.

You may need help through these steps. That is why I recommend a coach, mentor, or personal trainer to help you stay accountable.

The journey will be difficult in the beginning. Don't forget to rest and recharge.

You may encounter the following hurdles in your journey.

Negative thoughts will show up often, especially in the beginning. To combat them, you must reprogram your mind. Do not tell yourself that you "don't have time to work out," or that you are, "too tired." Instead, use positive and empowering thoughts. Remind yourself how much fun you have while working out. Tell yourself that you, "have plenty of energy to accomplish a satisfying workout." To get through this, continue using positive affirmations.

Disbelief in yourself will creep up on you. Instead, become a believer. Believe in the image of the future body you want to have. At first, you'll have to tell yourself the right stories to create motivation. You'll have to believe that you want that energy, you want to feel good, you want stamina, clarity, oxygen, and the body you have visualized. Create harmony between your body and mind.

You might experience a *lack of discipline*. Embrace discipline. Discipline is a skill that allows you to control and direct your mind, body, and soul. Master discipline by creating the habit of working out. Find a workout partner to keep you accountable.

Creating Your Workout Routine

Your workout should fit your lifestyle and your goals. It doesn't have to be a strict routine; it can be simple. But, make sure it's something you love. It can be anything, just as long as it keeps you moving and improves your strength. Plan out your workouts and keep them interesting.

There are so many kinds of exercise you can learn to enjoy, and it might change during various phases of your life. Basketball was my great love, though I don't play much now, since the players who match my size are younger and faster than me. I don't want to play and get hurt anymore, but cardio is still so much fun.

During my pregnancy, low impact aerobics and swimming were fantastic for me. I've done a little Bikram yoga—the hot yoga—a few times, but it was a bit too sweaty and time-consuming for me. I've taught aerobics in the past,

I've run, and I've played sports. I have always loved to lift weights, though, and I tease my friends that I will be ninety-two years old and in the gym lifting weights.

My point is, whatever it is, do what you love so it doesn't feel like work. If you don't love running on the treadmill, run on the beach or in the mountains. If you don't like lifting weights with a trainer, swim or do yoga, Zumba, dance or push-ups and pull-ups. When you find something you can embrace and learn to love, it isn't as difficult to keep going. But to find those things, you have to start with an open mind that says, "I've never tried this. Let me see how I like it."

Be open-minded to new forms of exercise. If you tell yourself you won't like something, you won't like it. Instead, be open to new things. Become an expert in them. Learn to do them quickly, beautifully, and well so they become rituals that enrich your life.

Your self-esteem and confidence will improve. After all, everything gets better when you like how you feel and look!

Challenge Others and Yourself

Within the real estate industry and in my circle of friends, we love to challenge ourselves. I am always up for a challenge. In fact, I'm usually the one pushing the younger agents toward a competition. My son told me just last year that in many ways (especially in my competitive nature), I am younger than he is.

One day, while I was at a convention, I went to the hotel gym to get a workout in. While there, I saw someone doing pull-ups. I thought, *I can do this*, and I went right for the bar to try to lift my chin over it. I couldn't do it! I made a goal of doing ten pull-ups by the next convention six months later, and I held myself accountable by sharing my goal with a friend of mine who is a top agent. He told me, "I'll do twenty by the next convention." Other people wanted to get in on the game, and by the end, it turned into a bet amongst six of us. The person who couldn't meet their goal would buy a bottle of Dom Perignon (about $220) for us to share during the next conference.

At the conference six months later, while we were all at the Four Seasons in Miami, I reached my goal. One of the guys couldn't reach his goal, and so we held him to the bet!

We weren't really competing against each other. Rather, we were challenging each other and holding each other accountable.

I wanted to lose five pounds recently, so, I declared on Facebook that I would only eat a salad for lunch, Monday through Friday, for a month and a half. I didn't have to tell anyone my weight goals or successes, but the declaration made it a challenge I felt obligated to complete. I blew through the challenge, and wouldn't you know, I enjoyed it so much I wound up eating salad sometimes on the weekends, too!

Everything Must Have a Plan

No matter what you want to do, answer three questions to make it happen: What do I want? Why do I want it? What actions do I need to take?

I filter every project, challenge, and assignment through those questions. They will build a very clear picture that I can leverage as motivation. Do you see how many times I repeat this process? Have you noticed?

Quitting Isn't an Option

Sometimes—whether from a lack of planning or an unclear objective to begin with—we find ourselves off track and overindulging in ways that do not serve us. The holidays sneak up on us and stress-eating takes over. Whatever the circumstances, too many people find themselves off track and then simply give up.

If you were traveling and got lost, would you simply throw

your keys away and quit moving? No. You'd check your GPS, find out where you went off track, identify the next turns, and then you'd keep driving. So, when you've had a huge meal that you hadn't planned, quitting doesn't serve you and your goals. When you overeat to the point of discomfort, you feel sick and weighed down. Instead, get right back to your schedule and plan.

So many people get off track and stay off track because they get discouraged when they make a mistake. These people are too hard on themselves. Getting healthy and working out, for instance, is more than just hard work; it is about your overall health benefits.

Don't focus on the size of your jeans. Instead, focus your energy on improving your health, stamina, and well-being, and the benefits of having more energy. The jeans will follow.

Plans, Not Diets

The more you know, the more you can prepare to avoid problems. You can cut down the learning curve. When I found out I was pregnant with my first child, I immediately bought several books and learned everything I could about having a baby. Then, I turned what I learned into a plan.

One of the things I learned was that pregnant women

should ideally gain twenty-five pounds while pregnant. The baby is usually about eight pounds, the placenta weighs a bit, the extra blood volume weighs a good amount, but that's really it. I expected to keep to that number.

As the pregnancy progressed, I craved certain foods—Concord grapes in particular, to the tune of two pounds of grapes every day! My husband had to shop for grapes all over town to keep up with my demand. They were just so ripe and sweet, and it felt so good to keep eating them. When I went in for my next appointment, the doctor told me I'd gained too much weight all at once.

Immediately, I pictured being weighed down after the pregnancy, dealing with everything that comes with the postpartum phase on top of being heavier than I would like. My doctor was excellent, though, and he told me, "Vanda, I'm glad you are making the right decisions for your health." And we made a plan to treat my body and the baby well. I ate good foods in good amounts and exercised right up until the baby was born, then again afterward as I was breastfeeding.

During both of my pregnancies, I gained around twenty-five pounds each time. I indulged some, but I didn't go crazy. On the flip side, I wasn't on a diet; I didn't count calories or restrict my eating. I had a plan and I stuck to it.

The point here is a plan is better than a diet. Decide what

your objectives are, plan to meet them, and stick to the plan. With a little planning and good discipline, you can make things happen.

We are animals, and animals often graze. They eat a bit here and a bit there. Our lifestyles have changed that for us, though. Many people eat twice a day, and they eat like crazy. Instead, go for a healthy breakfast with a small snack at 10:00 a.m., a light lunch, another snack at 3:00 p.m., and then dinner. Food should not bring your energy down. Eat often, eat light, eat healthy, organic, real, colorful foods in sensible qualities. Moderation is key.

Finally, be sure to drink plenty of water. Dehydration depletes your energy!

Breathing for Life and Energy

Oxygen is the most important thing in the world for us. Breathing is everything. The most important things for humans are oxygen, then water, then food. Sometimes, our fatigue and lack of physical energy comes from not breathing enough oxygen. A lack of oxygen can take your clarity and—because oxygen carries nutrients around in our blood—can make you tired, fatigued, and sick.

When your blood doesn't carry enough oxygen, it's hard for the cells to operate as they should. There is speculation that this might even cause some cells to mutate into cancer. Of course, it is not the only cause, but it is interesting to think about just how much impact breathing has on our bodies and our health.

This is another reason to prioritize exercise. When you exercise, you take in more oxygen and train your body to use it well.

Meditation is another great way to calm your mind and improve oxygen intake. When I meditate, I set aside fifteen minutes to focus on breath. You can create a rhythm by counting your breaths—five times in, five times out. During this practice, you are calming and grounding your mind as you focus on breathing. Your serotonin will get a boost, the immune system will grow stronger, your emotional and physical strength will grow, and it will all culminate in energy, clarity, calmness, and focus.

When stressed, most people immediately go to shallow breathing. This prevents oxygen from getting into your blood. When you feel yourself getting stressed, inhale, hold, and exhale. Do this ten times. I promise you will feel better.

What you do at the very end of the day is just as important as what you do in the beginning of it. That is because your before-bed routine sets you up for the morning ahead.

My nighttime ritual is important to me, and for that reason, I don't watch TV. Instead, I thank God for the beautiful day. I breathe. If I'm stressed, I say, "I now release," exhaling any doubt, anger, resentment, fear, and negative thoughts. I breathe in peace, calm, tranquility, love, gratitude, and strength. Lately, because I've practiced this routine so often, my body is automatically calm in the evenings so that I don't have to make it that way. That's where you want to be.

Train your mind and body long enough and the ritual will grant you the rest and rejuvenation you deserve.

CHAPTER 8

Silent Energy

———

"If you possess this inner quality, a calmness of mind, a degree of stability within, then even if you lack various external facilities that you would normally consider necessary for happiness, it is still possible to live a happy and joyful life."

—DALAI LAMA, IN *THE ART OF HAPPINESS*

Rest is so important. A deep sleep is transformative. A good power nap does wonders. It relaxes, rejuvenates, and empowers.

Guilt, Shame, and Expectations

In the US, there is a strange cultural fear of rest. People feel major guilt for taking breaks or going on vacation. They view people who take naps as weak. I recently watched a TED Talk about how sick Americans are becoming compared to the rest of the world, because they do not take breaks or rest enough.

This is ridiculous. We should work to live well, not live to work more. What kind of life is it to feel bad about taking time for yourself and your family?

The way we think people perceive us can limit us in so many ways. We wonder if we will need to apologize for taking the day off or explain why we were napping. A good friend of mine teases me when I step away for a quick nap or need another snack. She picks on me for taking naps and snacking. But, I do these things because I need to constantly restore my body. My energy levels buzz like a hummingbird. I give and give, but when I need to rest, I have to take the opportunity to do it or I will crash. A nap, or even a mindset break, can rejuvenate me to keep going the rest of the day at a much higher energy level.

Think about it. Are any of us productive when we are tired? I get cranky, irritable, and impatient. I'm no good for my kids, my clients, or myself. I would be a source of negativity because I would be impatient. I don't perform at the highest level and, sometimes, accidents can happen. A quick little nap can renew me, build my energy levels, and calm my nerves so I can perform at the highest levels once more. If you don't put gasoline in your car often enough, soon all you will get is a "puff-puff-puff" and a dead engine.

I don't know about you, but I want to be extraordinary. I want to press forward with high energy, great intensity, and unbroken focus. That intensity drains energy quickly. I want to fill my tank so I can be absolutely outstanding. Why feel guilty about something that makes you excel?

Resting Is Part of Work

When I lived in Los Angeles, a friend from Brazil asked me to host three Brazilian national-level marathon runners in my home. Runners don't often make a lot of money, so it was my pleasure to help them afford to come and compete. The runners stayed with me for three days. They practiced with great intensity every day. *Practice, practice, practice.* The day before the Los Angeles marathon, they didn't run at all. They practiced as long as they could, then rested to save their energy.

When I played basketball at the state level, we would practice for three hours twice a day to prepare for the national tournament. We conditioned ourselves, played against each other, and played against the guys. We were the best in the state and had no other competition. If the games were scheduled for a Sunday, we would practice for hours on Friday, then rest on Saturday. The day before a big tournament was always set aside for a little bit of conditioning and stretching, and a lot of rest and mental preparation. We recuperated, rested, and recharged.

These tools—recuperation, rest, and recharge—are just as important in the high-performance business world as they are in sports. If you don't allow yourself time to rest, you will only perform at mediocre levels. You'll never reach that outstanding level of mastery.

Resting versus Recharging

Recall that resting and recharging are different. Rest is when you sleep in, take a nap, or lay around the house in your pajamas. Rest is important. You've got to do it. Get that beauty rest!

On the other hand, recharging is just as necessary but comes from a different source. Most people don't understand the difference. They try to recharge themselves through rest, but they miss the point.

We recharge from joy, love, connection, and laughter. These are some of the purest emotions, and they cleanse your system of fears, regrets, and stress. They heal you.

Connection with the people you love may be the absolute best way to recharge. Vacation and holidays, when they are done right, leave us feeling so good afterward because we've been able to spend time laughing and enjoying the people we love. Connection with nature can have a similar effect, so I tell all my clients to go on vacation for at least ten days each year, with a long weekend every quarter.

The Consequences of Stress

You need to recharge in order to get energy. Rest is not enough because you might sleep eight hours a day and still find yourself lacking energy. Sometimes, that's because you are missing the connection and laughter that can recharge you. If you are sleeping eight hours a day and still feeling tired and without energy, unless there is a chemical imbalance to address, you are most likely resting without recharging.

Recharging refreshes and renews us. It revitalizes our mind and body.

I Didn't Rest or Recharge

When I was just three years into selling real estate, my determination and focus had already skyrocketed my success beyond my level of maturity. Emotionally, I was not prepared for the stress that came with that level of growth. People get stressed to the bone when they sell a house, and I was working with a lot of people selling their houses. Their stress really impacted me in ways I did not understand at the time.

In December of that year, I was invited to go to Vail, Colorado, for the holidays, where my friend lived. There is a common misconception that the real estate industry sleeps in December, but let me tell you, December was always my busiest month. During that particular December, I found myself just three years into the business, with nineteen homes under contract, waiting in escrow. Plus, I was dealing with the normal stress of the holiday season.

According to the National Association of Realtors, the average realtor sells four to five homes a year, and I was about to close seventeen homes between Christmas and New Year's alone. Five of those deals were part of a domino effect, where one had to work to make the next work, and so on. And, of course, I still wanted to make that trip work.

But, mentally, I was not prepared for that level of stress. I had no release techniques at the time. I wasn't emotionally strong at that point; I was still young and tense underneath all of the pressure. One night, my husband tried to help by getting dinner, and he went out and bought tortellini with tomato sauce.

No more than forty-five minutes after eating, I was in

the worst pain of my life. It felt like it could have been a heart attack—the worst pain I have ever felt. I arrived at the emergency room screaming. It felt as though my chest was on fire.

I had acute acid reflux. My stomach had become so full of acid amidst the stress and nervousness that the tomato sauce tipped me over the edge. They prescribed pills for the reflux and told me I'd be taking them the rest of my life. "There's nothing wrong with your lungs, heart, or stomach. Avoid stress and avoid acidic foods," they told me.

At that time, I had an epiphany. I realized I was taking care of my body and mind, but I wasn't taking care of my soul, emotional health, or spirit.

That's when I decided to make a change. I started to meditate. I decided to take more control of my focus and emotions and become stronger.

I'd been waking up in the middle of the night in a panic, thinking I had forgotten something or let something fall through the cracks. I'd taken on all of those clients' stress and wasn't mature enough to handle it in a healthy way. I had to decide not to let their fear, drama, and worries make me sick. I could be a problem solver without trying to work miracles. I'm not a magician. I decided I needed to not let their stress and fears affect me.

Five months later, I was able to stop taking the pills, thanks to release exercises, breathing, and disconnecting myself from those kinds of intense emotional circumstances. Today, I have shifted my focus so that drama and fears don't affect me.

Ferraris and Pintos

Some people take better care of their cars than they do themselves. They wash their cars and keep them in good shape. They change the oil regularly and keep the gas tank fueled. But, for some reason, they don't treat themselves nearly as well. They leave their minds and bodies by the wayside. They don't eat well, drink enough water, or exercise. They have no maintenance schedules or tune-ups.

We have to think of our bodies as a machine. I try to treat mine like a Ferrari, though some of you might only have a Pinto or a beat-up Hyundai right now. Shift your thinking. Fill your machine with plenty of water, good nutritious food that gives you energy, and then rest, recharge, and recuperate.

My ex used to tell me, "I admire you because you take the time to do the things you know are good for you." He would laugh when I would walk into the house and tell him I needed just a minute to recharge. Then, I would keep walking right into my room and lock the door for ten minutes or so. Hiding in my room for a little bit functioned as a decontamination chamber, allowing me to ground myself so that I had love and focus to give to my kids and my family. When I'm feeling down, I immediately start planning a trip. I look at pictures and envision the fun. I think about what I'm grateful for—the things I've done and the things I can plan to do. I know exactly what to do to shift my focus, and I can do it quickly.

My ex didn't know how to do this, and few people really do. They don't give their bodies the care they give external things. They don't take naps; they think massages are a waste time and money. They feel guilty taking a day off. Their thinking is mired in the idea that self-care is neither efficient nor effective.

Some people continue to wash, wax, and clean their cars while eating fast-food, sitting in a chair all day, and not breathing right. They carry their worries, guilt, complaints, regrets, shame, and anger, and then they wonder why they get sick or feel sluggish.

Perfect Is Boring

Stop thinking or wishing that you could be perfect. You just have to be the best you can be. Be great, don't be perfect! Perfection is impossible. Perfection is unattainable and boring. Be great, instead, and aim for constant improvement and growth.

But, be wary: good is the enemy of great. There's always a higher level, always a better place to go. All I ask is that you not stay complacent. Complacency takes energy away, draining passion, enthusiasm, and joy. Complacency is one of the biggest killers of human potential and high energy.

Rock your boat often, challenge yourself often. Keep your environment exciting.

Tools to Rejuvenate

I use the following tools when I want to rejuvenate.

Mindset Break

Create the habit of putting aside ten minutes a day at specific times to have a mindset break. Do this at least twice a day. We feed our bodies three times a day, sometimes more. Why not feed your mind and soul multiple times a day? Find a quiet place, unplug, and regroup. Visualize your short-term goals for the day. Check in with yourself. Do you need to step outside and breathe? Do you need to eat something healthy? Do you need a hit of endorphins? But first, do some even breathing to stop the noise and distractions in your head so you can refocus.

Smile and Have Fun

The quickest way to rejuvenate and adjust your mindset is to laugh and experience joy. It's fun. It's healing. Laughing makes you look better and feel better. People will laugh with you and want to be around you, which is good for business, life, and health.

Your brain is listening, remember? It has no idea if what you are saying or doing is a joke or a command. It's just waiting for your instruction. Your brain will change based on what you say and how you act because of its plasticity. When you affirm laughter and joy, your brain conforms to it.

The brain registers the act of smiling as happiness.

Meditation

You should devote twenty or thirty minutes every day to meditation. Set aside that time to get to a quiet place, still the mind, and breathe deeply. When I was under a great deal of stress, my doctor recommended that I meditate twice daily. Now, I meditate once, usually in the mornings.

Meditation is essential because it is a mental workout that can contribute to strength, energy, and focus, as any physical workout can.

My meditation routine is simple. I find a place to sit down

comfortably. I relax my legs, put my hands on my lap, and close my eyes. I focus on breathing and emptying my brain. I say four affirmations. Then, I slow down my body and mind. I take eight deep breaths to get myself in the quiet zone. While meditating, I don't want to hear my thoughts rattling around. When a thought comes in, I work to push it away and focus more on my breathing.

Stimulation, noise, and busyness is the normal state for many people. They turn on the TV while they work, and they listen to music when they read. We are used to noise, and it can be difficult to adjust to quietness. So, if you've never meditated or you don't make it a practice, twenty minutes of controlling your mind and breath in silence can feel like an eternity. Be patient. It will get easier. Start small as you experiment with the meditation style that works for you. All I require of you is to find a time without interruption. Start small. Five minutes is plenty to begin to learn how to bring oxygen into your body and stillness to your mind.

One time, when I went to the spa for a facial, the girl who worked on me told me about a silent retreat that she had just experienced. She spent a full week in complete silence. At the retreat, every moment of her day was on a schedule. Participants woke up early, meditated, completed chores, walked, meditated more, completed more chores, and went to bed early. She said the first days were difficult, but soon, her body and mind got used to it. *Silence. No talking.*

This is an excellent example of how silence and meditation can fit into a productive schedule. Our objective is to bring those moments of grounded silence into our existing lives to make our daily existence more peaceful and more enjoyable!

CHAPTER 9

Love, Joy, and Fun Energy

———

*"The secret of staying young is to live honestly,
eat slowly, and lie about your age."*

—LUCILLE BALL

To create the level of energy you want, you must first
understand the central role of love, joy, and fun in a successful life.

The Source of Positive Energy

Two strong sources of positive energy are love and joy.
They are connected; when you have love, you have joy.
Love is one of the strongest, clearest, and most powerful
emotions. You are stronger when you love and are loved.
When you love, you are more grateful, giving, caring, and

compassionate. Together with joy and gratitude, love enables you to form the strongest connections to people and to the world.

To house these positive emotions, we must release other emotions that weigh us down.

Use the Energy of Love

You can use the energy of love to better your life and the lives of the people around you, but first, you have to love yourself. Self-love improves and increases your self-esteem. The better you see yourself, the more positively you will view the future, and the better you will feel.

Once you love yourself, you can share love unconditionally. You must learn to give positive energy even to those you don't like.

A Culture of Celebration

Brazil has a reputation for being a place where people sing and dance and parties overflow into the streets. Brazilians have a certain *joie de vivre*. We are youthful, fun, and energetic people, and it has become an ingrained aspect of our culture.

Grandmothers and grandfathers teach their children and

grandchildren how to come together, celebrate, and enjoy life. And of course, it doesn't hurt that we have the warm sun and beautiful beaches!

But like any place, there are negative, unhappy people as well. Regardless of where you are, you still have to choose love, joy, gratitude, and connection.

I had a lot of challenges growing up, but I decided at an early age to focus on the good—*good things, good energy, good emotions.* If I look back, I remember every year of my life being filled with joy, fun, and happiness. There were difficult times there, of course, but Brazilians make time for fun and family to help them through the rough patches. In this way, fun and family create joy even in difficult circumstances.

I return to Brazil once a year to rejuvenate as much as I can.

Giving from What We Have

If you don't rejuvenate and fill up your own bucket, you have nothing to pour out for other people. Build up your stores of love, joy, passion, enthusiasm, and optimism. Fill your heart, mind, and soul with these good things so you can give to others. In turn, you will keep receiving more good things.

Life feels lousy sometimes, and few of us ever realize that

it may be that way because we spend all our time focusing on lousy things. We dwell on bad feelings, think and share negative thoughts, and then wonder why negativity surrounds us.

We ask the universe to *give me, give me* all these things, and in return, the universe also says *give me, give me*, which means it is taking from us.

Instead, we should be the ones giving. We should be saying, "Here, take it, take it." In turn, the universe will say, "Here, take it, take it. It's yours!"

Thinking in this way will generate abundance in your life. Prepare yourself to be able to share feel-good emotions, love, good thoughts, and it will come back to you multiplied.

I don't have to love everyone, but I can choose not to hate them. I can choose to embrace love, joy, passion, and gratitude no matter who is around me. I can limit the amount of time I spend around those people and refrain from pouring judgment and criticism on them when they do come around.

We can only give the things that we foster within ourselves. If my love and joy are pure, when I am squeezed and tested, love and joy will come from me, like orange juice from an orange.

It's easy to love the people who love you. It is hard to love someone you don't know or who doesn't love you back.

When my boys misbehaved as children, I didn't love their behavior, but I still loved them. I learned to separate the behavior from the person.

Unconditional love purifies the energy in your soul—it is a necessary ingredient to a high-energy life.

Humor Is Important

Humor is a component of love. Humor is a game changer. It breaks patterns and releases energy blocks. I've heard humor and laughter being used as a treatment for severe illness. Just look at the evidence: happy people live five to ten years longer than anybody else. Your cells even change as you laugh, renewing your body from a molecular level.

Laughter really is the best medicine!

Studies have shown a child laughs 156 times per day. An adult laughs only three times per day. That is so depressing to me!

Experiencing humor increases our energy and feeling of well-being. Humor keeps us open and relaxed. It helps our energy flow better, which gives us more clarity and focus to help us make better decisions. We are more flexible when we can laugh at ourselves.

Schedule some laughter into your day! *Chillax*! No one makes it out alive anyways! We might as well have some fun in the process!

Wearing Joy Like a Coat

Joy goes hand in hand with love and gratitude as a powerful, healing emotion. It comes easier in some phases of life than others.

Joy and gratitude super-boost our energy. When life gets crazy—stress, drama, worries, and problems—learn how to step into that place of joy. Tell those around you, "Okay, I'll be right back. I need a moment," then step into a closed office or your car, close your eyes, and visualize yourself in that place of joy. Focus on your gratitude in that moment.

For example, I sometimes return to the days when my boys were born. When I first held Peter in my arms, I was filled with so much joy. I was wired with love and energy. It was so physically tangible, I felt as though I was vibrating. When I return to that moment and recall how my heart felt full in my chest—I can feel it again.

Sometimes, I remember a special moment that I had with my lovely mom whom I miss so much.

You can learn how to get yourself into the mindset of joy, regardless of the moment. All you have to do is flex your happy muscle and find your happy place. It is simple to do, but we somehow manage to complicate the process. Do you have a happy place in your mind?

We can flex our happiness muscle with an example that I am sure everyone can relate to. Imagine your last beach vacation. Imagine putting your feet in the white sand and listening to the calm ocean lapping at the shore. See the deep blues and greens of the water and feel the warm sun and gentle breeze. Breathe deeply as though you're breathing in the salty sea air. Find that place that brings you joy so you can go there whenever the stress and drama get to be too much.

If you don't like the beach or have never been, picture yourself amongst a group of friends. Remember how good it feels to be talking with people whom you love and care for. Remember how it feels to be connected and understood. Feel the joy you have when you spend time with them.

When you learn how to find a feeling of joy regardless of circumstance, it's almost like putting on a coat. Wear it when you need that burst of joy and happiness.

That joy will create positive energy, and that positive energy will lead to success.

Grown Up, Rich, and Miserable

Let me ask you something, have you ever seen a pessimistic toddler? Do you know any little babies who carry baggage? No. Children have to learn how to worry. They aren't born with negative thoughts. Their moms, dads, uncles, aunts, teachers, friends, and everyone around them imparts negativity and worry onto them: *You're going to get hurt. You can't do this. You're too small for that.* But toddlers believe they can do anything. They have pure joy, enthusiasm, and determination.

Children are innocent, and much of that innocence extends even into the teenage years. Think about how much teenagers giggle and joke. I've raised my two boys, and I housed eight other nieces and nephews through their teenage years. Those kids giggled all the time—they were so excited! They enjoyed life without the worry of bills and the stressors of life.

The more responsibilities we have, the crankier we seem to become. It's as though we feel like being serious helps to pay the bills. You have to look the part, or look like you know what you're doing.

I've seen a lot of successful people who were stiff, serious, and miserable. I'm sure you know at least one successful, but negative son-of-a-gun. Although they are successful, they aren't living right.

The secret to living well is to have success and joy.

Too many successful, beautiful, rich, famous people have committed suicide. Wealth does not fill any voids. In fact, when I observed successful people and their energy back in Brazil, money wasn't even a thought. The people I noticed were simply contagious. They were fun, engaging, happy, and optimistic. The money didn't matter, but the joy did!

Conscious Joy

Sometimes you will be happy, other times you will fluctuate in and out of happiness. That is okay. What I want you to work on is conditioning yourself and your mind so that when you feel sad, bad, or miserable, you know how to respond to get yourself back to equilibrium. It *is* possible to consciously find joy and place yourself in a state of energy.

Listen, the only place where everything is perfectly balanced is the cemetery. Life is not balanced. Life comes and goes like the waves of the ocean. Life is beautifully imperfect. Embrace it with love, joy, gratitude, and the laughter of a child.

CHAPTER 10

Consistent Energy

———

"We are what we repeatedly do. Excellence, then, is not an act but a habit."

—ARISTOTLE

People often ask me how I keep my energy high on such a consistent basis. I tell them that first, I have made the choice to be committed to having positive, high energy. Every day, I ask myself, "Vanda, will you be in a high-energy state today or will you be average?" Every single day, I choose to have high energy.

I am always ready, open, and flexible, especially when dealing with energy blocks. If I find myself struggling in some way—with sadness, nostalgia, worry, or sluggishness—I recognize it immediately as something outside of my chosen state of high energy or emotion. Then, I immediately change my focus and regain my energy.

Affirmations are a huge help when overcoming setbacks. I tell myself, "I'm strong, healthy, and powerful. I learn fast and I can learn anything I want."

Sometimes, we all find ourselves hitting snooze on our alarm clocks. But, we can't do that! We have to get up and face the day! We have to create a mindset and outlook that will raise our energy to help us get out of bed.

Every single morning, I wake up with the desire and the intention for energy and enthusiasm. I put myself in the zone that way, and because I do it every single morning, I have confidence that I can do it again and again.

Because of the repetition of practicing this every day, I've made high energy into a habit.

Repetition, Practice, and Intention

The more you practice something, the better you become at it. Repetition is a discipline we can use to move us forward toward our goals.

Intentional, repetitive practice is the key to learning and getting stuff done.

I practice having high energy every single day and now it has become a habit. Because I have a habit of doing the things that will help me keep my high energy, the decisions I need to get there come easier for me.

In creating positive habits that lend themselves to high energy, you must have mental discipline. That is because habits require consistency. I believe it takes about ninety days to create a strong habit. So, you have to be consistent in your action for a while before your body and mind can recognize the pattern. I believe that your habit is ingrained once your body misses it when you stop doing it. For instance, if you make it a habit to run every day, and then you suddenly stop, your legs yearn for movement.

Research has shown it is easier to create a new habit by linking it to an already ingrained habit. If you want to drink more water, attach it to a habit you already have. For instance, you could attach it to your habit of getting up to go get a cup of coffee in the breakroom. Every time you drink a cup of coffee, also drink a cup of water. Attaching these two habits together links them and creates a ritual. Once you practice the ritual of pouring yourself a cup of water every time you pour yourself a cup of coffee, the habit of drinking water will be ingrained.

Getting to that point, however, is difficult because you have to get past the hurdle of not wanting to do the hard work to create the habit. To get around that initial struggle, surround your new habits with positive, fun emotions.

Just remember that feelings control your perception. So, if you have a happy feeling while creating a habit, your perception will be rosier. For instance, if you are trying to get in the habit of running, bring your dog along! Seeing how happy the fresh air and activity makes him will in turn make you have a joyous feeling when you take him running. You will be able to set the habit more easily.

Don't be too hard on yourself. It is difficult to have a positive outlook at first. You can't control negative thoughts that pop into your head. They just happen. But, you can control how you respond to them. You can't let those negative thoughts tumble around in your head for long. Get rid of them, so they don't control your perception.

What Zen Masters Know about Rituals

When my boys' father was living in Maui, Hawaii, every day he would hear a bell ring at a specific time. After several days of noticing this pattern, he got curious. "What could the bell be for?" he wondered. So, he decided to go for a walk to find where the sound of the ringing bell was coming from. Turns out, the bell was housed in a Zen center. The bell tolled to inform the people at the Zen center when their daily rituals began and ended.

My ex-husband became friends with the Zen master, and he decided to join in their routines. He would meditate with them and care for the gardens. During this time, he learned how rituals brought peace to his day.

From him, I learned that when you have that kind of structure in your day, you feel more in control of it. You won't find yourself floating around, lost in whatever you're doing and caught up in the things that are looming.

Clients sometimes tell me they don't want a ritualized schedule at all, because they want to be free to do what they want. The reality is that a lack of structure feels even more constricting. I feel rather unsettled, wondering whether I've missed something or should be meeting another obligation. I'd rather have the structure to know that I can focus completely on a task without wondering what I'm missing. Chaos and confusion are not fun.

Your schedule is the map to the diamonds, and that includes planning fun and enjoyment into your day. Listen to music, watch something fun, break the pattern with humor and joy. These are the things that can keep the schedule enjoyable, so you can keep following it.

Building Discipline

To build habits, you must build discipline. We need discipline because it helps us accomplish what we have to accomplish, even when we don't feel like it. It also helps us finish what we start. Discipline helps us build patience and it also makes us mentally tough. Through discipline, we can remove mental and physical distractions.

When you master basic skills or learn to discipline yourself, you build strength and confidence. With that certainty, you can move on to master one skill and then another. In this way, everything is connected. When I coach people to train their mindset, improve their focus, and raise their energy to build their business, ripples are set into motion.

When you improve yourself in one way, everything else begins to improve, as well—much like a ripple effect.

Balance Your Focus

To maintain your sense of balance, remember that life is a marathon, not a sprint.

Hope for the best but prepare for the worst. You can't go wrong with that mindset! Come from a place of positivity, but prepare to be tested. Meet those tests with commitment, faith, and a willingness to go the extra mile.

Believe in yourself so you can reach the finish line. Get there with weekly accountability.

Allow yourself time for fun and learning. Balance that with work and your pursuit of mastery.

Balance Is Difficult, Don't Get Frustrated

Passionate people get out of balance quickly because they intensely focus on one thing. Understand this and do your best as you strive for harmony and energy in all areas.

I often see imbalance come about when we try to improve one area of our life, but let the others fall to the wayside. For instance, I've seen some people become obsessive exercisers to the detriment of their family and careers. This is a recipe for disaster.

Live Life on Purpose

Create a life with intention. *On purpose.*

Separate the various areas of focus in your life so you can work to maintain the balance. If you can work on a little of everything consistently, you can grow in each area toward a more balanced life.

Without a strong belief, a great plan, clear, specific goals, and focused intention, you're leaving your life up to chance.

Settle in for the long-term. You're going to be working

at this for decades. Be patient. Living an inspired, energetic life just takes time. Anything worthwhile does. Live every day like it's your last. Put all your energy into every moment!

Conclusion

In my eyes, living an extraordinary, energetic lifestyle means you are intentionally living the lifestyle that you want. It gives you love, joy, connection, fun, and peace of mind.

My extraordinary lifestyle will look different than your extraordinary lifestyle. If I envision $3,000,000 in savings, a couple of passive income properties, a beautiful place on the beach, a healthy family, and a wonderful, caring partner, I might consider myself happy. My blueprint will have been realized. But, that may not be your ideal.

Sometimes, people find themselves living a "great" lifestyle—they're rich, successful, famous—yet, they are still unhappy because they are living someone else's ideal or their life doesn't feel fulfilled.

You Get to Choose

The ideal lifestyle is to be able to do what you want, when you want, the way you want, anytime you want, and to do those things with the people you love. To one person, that might mean a small house in St. John's. To another, it might mean living in Manhattan and spending time seeing shows, going to the opera, and eating at nice restaurants.

So, what makes you happy?

I can't answer that for you, and I won't even try.

You get to choose. How you think, how you speak, how you eat and drink, how you act, how you interact with people, and how you live is all up to you. You get to decide what you're building toward and whether you make it there. This is about what you do want, not what you should want.

Listen, happiness has nothing to do with outside influences. You don't have to be given anything or have achieved your dream before you can be happy. You can be happy in the pursuit. Don't wait for everything to be perfect before you choose happiness.

Change What You Can, Accept What You Can't

In this journey of improvement, don't forget to accept

yourself. We are all different and unique, and you must come to love and accept yourself as who you are. Build your self-esteem, and with it will come confidence, consistency, and the foundations for an enjoyable life.

There are some things you can't change, and that's okay. I don't have a supermodel's body and, no matter what, I will never be able to be five-foot-nine! I accept that!

Instead of wishing you were someone or something else, look for ways that you can be a better *you*. In order to do this, it helps to follow the paths that successful people have trodden before you. Anything you want to do has already been done in some way. All you have to do is emulate it to be your better self! Find the best in your field and be more like them. If they did it, so can you! You might even be able to do it better!

Happiness is progression. If I were to hand you everything you want right now, but you remained stagnant, eventually you would become unhappy. Instead, strive to always improve. Improve yourself, your lifestyle, and the people around you.

Reverse Engineer Your Life for Extraordinary Energy

Know what you want? Good. Now open your phone and start creating a schedule.

Don't wake up in the morning wondering what you're going to do, where you're going to go, or what you even want in the first place. That's an unproductive and stressful way to live your life. Schedule the actions, schedule the fun, schedule the work. Schedule the joy. Schedule the energy.

If you don't make a plan, someone else will put you on theirs. You don't want that. You want to live your own life.

Plan your day. Plan your month. Plan your year—three years out, five years out, ten years out. Plan it all, because time moves too fast as it is. You don't want to live life by accident.

Start with your goal for ten years from now and work backward. What will you need to have accomplished by then? What needs to happen by five years? Three? Keep breaking it down until you know what you need to do every year in order to reach that goal.

People are often surprised when their goals become attainable in this way. But, that is my job. I work to make it simple for you. I work to help you see the potential for a big dream and then make it happen by keeping you accountable and focusing you on feasible goals.

I'm on a mission to see you succeed, darling. I'm on a

mission to change your life and the lives of others. Your success, whatever it means to you, is part of my mission. Join my mission, gain an amazing level of energy, and find out what your life will become.

High energy is a powerful choice. Decide to have it.

Use your personal energy as a tool to achieve your dreams. Use it as a shield, a sword to protect your strength and passion. Use it for all it is worth.

As you attain a high and beautiful state of being, you can create, generate, nurture, and share your energy throughout this lovely universe.

Give your energy to others. We need more people like you!

With love and high energy to you!

Love, Vanda.

Affirmations

I am active, energetic, healthy,
strong, wealthy, and happy.

I am fit, beautiful, and full of life.

I am strong, positive, enthusiastic, and powerful.

I am a person who enjoys and appreciates
life every day. I do things constantly
to improve my life to the next level of
health, wisdom, joy, and success.

Every day, I get up early knowing there is so
much to learn and enjoy, so many fun things
to do, and so much money out there to earn.

My day is planned well. I eat well and healthy. I have daily workouts that keep me healthy, and I am productive.

I look at everything and everyone from an optimistic point of view and I expect only the best of every situation.

I only speak in very positive terms. I control my thoughts so there is no room for any negative thoughts.

I am passionate and follow my dreams.

I am grateful for my achievements.

I smile with confidence. I am going in the right direction and I am doing my part to get there.

I am an inspiration to all the people around me, and I am always willing to help.

I take time every day to recharge myself. I use visualization and meditation techniques to do this.

Other people are very attracted to me because I have such beautiful, high energy. I work to surround myself with people of the same energy.

All my relationships are exciting, inspiring, and I feel fulfilled. People love me, and I love them back.

I am like a magnet! I am irresistible!

I keep myself in a state of high energy, confidence, beauty, and grace.

Everyone can see that I am happy, strong, and certain about my bright future.

I always avoid negative emotions.

I protect my energy and energy field; therefore, my environment is pure.

I share my positive energy with everyone, because the more I give, the more I receive!

I give back to the universe with a smile by sharing, supporting, working, dreaming, giving, and believing in myself and others.

The new ME is fit and more beautiful than ever before.

When people are around me, they feel lighter and more enthusiastic because I am inspiring.

I take time to take care of myself daily.

*I keep my energy tank full at all
times, and I protect myself from energy
suckers and negative people.*

I am powerful, positive, and a very strong person.

*I eat the right food and that increases
my energy and well-being.*

I am in control of what I allow into my mind.

*Abundance is a natural state for me. Wealth
is my natural state. Joy is my natural state.*

My energy is beautiful.

*I live in a state of gratitude. I am completely
grateful for everything and everyone in my life.*

About the Author

Vanda Martin has lived a varied and full life: earning a basketball scholarship, owning her first enterprise at nineteen, obtaining a degree in business and marketing, moving to the United States from Brazil, working as a personal trainer, becoming the number-one realtor in her region and part of the top 1 percent worldwide with Coldwell Banker, and finally becoming a successful coach. In 2006, she was named "Business Woman of the Year" by the San Joaquin County Chamber of Commerce. It is all thanks to her mindset, focus, love of life, and drive to maintain high energy. Vanda lives in northern California and has two sons.

Made in the USA
Middletown, DE
30 December 2017